ROBERT SCHULLER

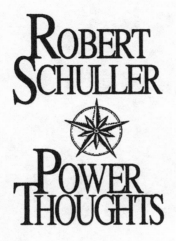

POWER THOUGHTS

ROBERT SCHULLER

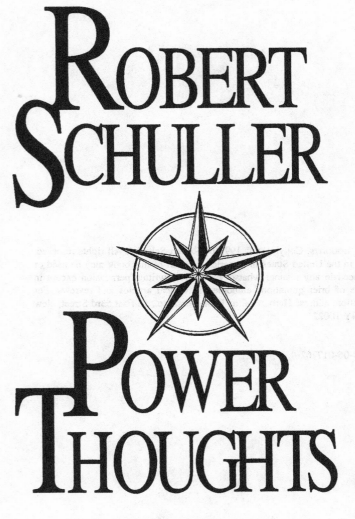

POWER THOUGHTS

Achieve Your True Potential
Through Power Thinking

HarperCollins*Publishers*

ISBN 0-06-017762-4

This book
is proudly and affectionately
Dedicated
to
Five Beautiful Families
– my five children, –
– their spouses, –
All of whom have beautiful
Christian Marriages!
– And their children –
My sixteen Grandchildren:

Christina Schuller
Bobby Schuller
Angie Schuller
Anthony John Schuller
Jason Coleman
Christopher Coleman
Scott Coleman
Nicky Coleman
Jennifer Dunn
Stephanie Dunn
David Dunn
Rebekah Milner
Ethan Milner
Timothy Milner
Julia Penner
Paige Penner

All of whom will have the glorious experience of living
in the twenty-first century as Power Thinkers making a
difference.

Acknowledgments

This book would not be possible without the skilled team of editors, word processors, technicians, typists and my family who assisted me.

Thank you, each and every one.

Most of all, this book would not have been possible without the Power Thinkers whose wisdom and personal testimonies have empowered me and hopefully will empower you as you read these pages.

Contents

Contents

ROBERT SCHULLER

POWER THOUGHTS

1

The Greatest
Power Thought
of All

$\mathbf{I}$n the beginning ... !?

Dinosaurs?

Some time ago, I was seated at a dinner with George Lucas, whom you undoubtedly know was the creator of *Star Wars*. He told me he was working on a new movie with Steven Spielberg about dinosaurs. The next day I chatted with the world-famous dinosaur authority Dr. John Horner from the University of Montana.

Sometime later I went to see *Jurassic Park*, and it blew me away. The age-old questions dominated my thoughts: How long has the <u>universe</u> been here? 60 million years? 120 million years? 230 million years? Scientists estimate the earth is at least four and a half billion years old.

Was there always <u>something</u> here?

<u>Once</u> there was <u>nothing</u>?!

What a thought: From <u>nothing</u> to Galaxies? Millions of creatures—still living!—survivors who have escaped extinction? Today in this computer-chip age, this new genetic research era, this explosive time of incredible human creativity with all its fabulous collective resources, known and unknown; scientific and psychological; material and spiritual; discovered and still unimagined but <u>real</u>?

All of THIS out of NOTHING?

You want a Super Power Thought? Try that one for a starter.

Hard to accept, you say? It is impossible to handle this idea without the magnificent assumption called FAITH!

How did that first, yes, the very first <u>something</u> out of <u>nothing</u> get started? Chemical mix you say? But where did the "chemicals" come from?

Energy generated by light? But where did the LIGHT come from?

How could <u>something</u> come out of <u>nothing</u>?

A Big Bang? But where did that <u>first</u> energy <u>come from</u>?

Yes!! Of course. <u>Ideas</u> generate energy!

"In the beginning" . . . there was a <u>Super</u> <u>POWER</u> <u>THOUGHT!</u>

The Awesome Power of a Silent Thought!

Did it make any sound when this first, great Power Thought created something out of nothing? Was there a Big Bang? Like sixty million thermonuclear explosions in one, never-to-be-matched or imagined sound?

Or did it start in sublime, sacred silence, in a stillness so awesome that the silence thundered out the consciousness of the ultimate reality—GOD?

GOD! What a creative Thought!

What a powerful, soundless Reality!

There is Awesome stillness in the power places where real creativity happens;

in sublime centers of silence
where no human being has ever walked, breathed,
listened or looked.
Just look at the power encapsulated
in The Soundless Centers of Creation:

Sperm connects with egg.
Idea penetrates consciousness.
Thought enters brain.
Power is turned on!
IGNITION!

Someone, somewhere pushed a button
connecting creative energies and
suddenly, silently there is:
    Light out of darkness.
      Life out of death.
        Something out of nothing!

3

What happened? Who did it? Where will it lead? What has been born? What has been released? What is its destiny? How long will it last? Can it ever be terminated?

THE FIRST GREAT POWER THOUGHT

Once there was nothing—then there was something.
And this something became something more: Elements, water, air, fire.
And this something more became everything.
Atoms, genes, molecules, amoebas, dinosaurs.
Plans evolved, genetic blueprints, D.N.A.
What has this Ultimate Intelligence Power Thought wrought?
Hummingbirds and eagles.
Mice and men.
Lice and lions.
Bacteria, butterflies and buffalo.
And this something more became everything.

ECOLOGICAL ARCHITECTURE!

This boggles the human imagination. Every thing, every creature, every living life force, has a perfectly powerful part to play in the divine drama that has surely, slowly, silently, splendidly, stunningly unfolded. "God is in the details," the great architect Ludwig Mies van der Rohe said.

4

Look at this great Power Thought unfolding.
Shh . . . Be quiet! Don't say a word.
Just look and listen to the creative silence.
Witness God at work.
What a spiritual, sacred, systematic scheme is emerging.

THE POWER THOUGHT CALLED YOU

Is there a plan, an ultimate purpose that the creative idea is destined to fulfill?

When something came from nothing, what was really created?

What will this creativity reproduce generation after generation after generation after generation?

What life force has been released?

Where will this road lead?

Watch the Ultimate Power Thought express itself through a daring, bold move to form and generate independent, intelligent energy systems. These energy systems will be replicated in multiplied billions—marvelous miniature reproductions of that Original Ultimate Intelligence.

These creatures will be called . . .

Homo sapiens . . .

Human beings . . .

Persons . . .

Thinking Creatures!

Beautiful spiritual instruments designed to

receive and

process dynamic data, and

generate creative ideas!

Yes, this force has created a human being . . . called YOU.

<u>You</u> and I are one of God's POWER THOUGHTS designed to be a power-thinking person.

Wow!! W.O.W.—<u>W</u>onder <u>O</u>f <u>W</u>onders!

You and I have the distinctive quality to "Believe." We have the immense ability to "comprehend God." We are able to feel the invisible presence of the Original Power Thinker! The Eternal Intelligent Energy Force. Some call this power "God." Alcoholics Anonymous choose "Higher Power." I know Him through a life called "Jesus."

Years ago I was a passenger on a chartered flight from New York City to Madrid, Spain. All of us were on our way to the World Psychiatric Congress. Next to me sat a Jewish doctor. She was a woman in her middle thirties, very intelligent and very dedicated.

"Do you believe in God?" I asked.

"Oh, yes!" she answered, explaining, "At medical school in Warsaw, Poland, we were taught 'Man is the only animal that has the capacity to comprehend God!'"

What a POWER THOUGHT! What an incredible possibility.

You are not only one of God's most carefully and darefully designed creatures, not only one of the strongest, brightest, and best of all creation, you are also the only creature able to know and comprehend God!

Yes,

<u>You</u> are <u>a</u> <u>miracle</u>!

You are a survivor! You escaped extinction.

You are an amazing and miraculous overcomer.

Yes, once there was an act of love. Millions of sperm were released. One, <u>only</u> <u>one</u> <u>survived</u> to connect with an egg. <u>You</u> were born. Congratulations!! Welcome to the human race, Power Thinker! Let the Power Thinking continue . . . in you!

What is power?

I'm writing this where I write all of my books—in a hideaway place. Less than one thousand feet from where I sit, the President of the United States is, as I'm writing this, sleeping, reading, talking, listening, eating—in his presidential suite on the ninth floor of the hotel. If I wanted to, I could walk on the front lawn, look up and perhaps see him on the balcony. Security people are everywhere trying to look inconspicuous, but the beepers they wear give them away. Nearly twenty police officers with as many black-and-white bikes are waiting to escort him at a moment's notice.

He has been my next-door neighbor for a few days. I feel power vibrating in the excitement of his presence.

Power—do YOU have it?

You can tell if people

return your phone calls,

send you a handwritten thank-you note,

invite you to their private party.

You begin to wonder

if you hear nothing, or

hear it secondhand, or

get a form letter in the mail.

But that's the category most of us fall in, right?

But wait a minute!

You've got great potential! So do I!

Because YOU can think POWER THOUGHTS.

Yes, they will come, out of the blue!

Power Thoughts are about to be born in your head and heart.

That great idea just may be the Presence of God entering into your personality.

You?—A Power Thinker?

Absolutely!

That, in itself, is a Power Thought!

Every positive idea has potentially infinite Possibilities. The taproot, the seminal source, the fertile seed of all creativity that generates productivity is an idea!

Yes, anyone can count the seeds in an apple, but only God can count all the apples in one seed. Think of all the apples that are waiting to evolve—

Orchards,

and factories,

and business for truckers,

and clients for accountants,

Jobs!

And tax dollars for the state and nation,

the possibilities go on and on and on . . .

all out of one seed in one apple!

Here's a Super Power Thought for you! The greatest power in the world is the power of a positive pregnant Idea!

"Oh, no!" someone replies, "God is the Greatest Power in the world."

"Of course," I agree, and I ask, "But what is God? How does He create life? And improve life?"

Some of you may answer, "Through Nature, genetic

8

systems, through evolution without outside intervention." I reply, "Not quite! Let me tell you a story I heard as a farm boy in Iowa. The pastor called on one of his farmer parishioners and said, 'Look what the Lord has done—what a beautiful farm! What straight rows of corn! What beautiful acres of grain!' To which the farmer replied, 'Yes, Pastor, but you should have seen it when the Lord had it all by Himself.'"

Yes—cancer will be cured someday.

Genetic research will mix and match marvelous genetic recipes
- to heal the sick,
- feed the hungry
- and allow humans to live longer lives,

cured from the ancient plagues of pitiful aging.

"Look what science has accomplished," secularists will declare.

"Yes," I add, "look what humans and God have done together!"

A creative idea in a human brain may be the Spirit of the Eternal God using his most exciting invention—the human mind! The human creature with a divinely designed built-in computer system! With a mind copied after the Original Idea-Generating Mind itself!

When these systems—human and Divine—connect, then amazing creative communication happens!

Watch out, world!

An awesome spiritual data-processing network truly exists in this infinite universe and is turned on right now!

What a system! W.O.W.!!! Wonder Of Wonders!

9

God is now
  living in you, and
  thinking through you—
  processing creative data using you!
What an amazing computer you are.
More than a "word" processor.

YOU ARE A "POWER THOUGHT" PROCESSOR.

Imagine yourself!
You are a computer that can
  Think!
  Judge,
  Choose,
  Decide,
  Feel!
Now consider, a computer that has this powerful human spirit called Ego.

But can this glorious computer called Man or Woman be trusted with all this potential power? Can this creature be trusted with the awesome power of Power Thinking? YES, if redeemed!

For this Power Thought Processor called a person is designed with a soul.

This "computer" is the only creature capable of making a decision to love and be love.

That's YOU!

Yes. You are a divine creature—an Eternal Soul.

W.O.W.!

Wonder Of Wonders!

10

Power Thinker!

That's what you are!

Power Thinking!

That's what you are designed for.

Now, you are ready to meet the living proof of what I have written.

Meet my friends.

I want you to meet the great men and women who are shaping the twenty-first century, because you are destined to run with that enthusiastic crowd, mix with those creative minds, and blend with those big-spirited persons.

These power thinkers are persons of marvelous and magnificent achievement.

They leave monuments behind

skyscrapers,

satellites,

new inventions to explore space,

lasers to probe the human body,

the discovery of physiological and spiritual truths that heal troubled lives.

Power thinkers. History is shaped by these courageous souls. The human race is rescued by these big-thinking people.

They are not all rich and famous. More often they are simple, sweet, sincere, unselfish souls with big hearts and a tender touch. Their eyes become misty easily and unashamedly when they offer caring love to another person.

Power-thinking people are the noble achievers. They are the men and women of success that command a standing ovation.

11

In 1993, a handful of people were chosen to receive America's "Hero Award." One of those rare and privileged persons was a woman who is called by her friends "Sweet Alice."

That honor was quickly followed by the "Essence Award," which is bestowed on African-American women. Besides Sweet Alice, the 1993 recipients included such outstanding women as Carol Moseley Braun, the first African-American woman elected to the U.S. Senate; Gail Deavers, the U.S. Olympic Gold Medalist; Aretha Franklin, the multi-Grammy award winner; Tina Turner; Rosa Parks.

Sweet Alice, a dear friend of mine, agreed to be interviewed on "Hour of Power." I looked at this vivacious woman with the infectious smile and said, "Is it true, Sweet Alice, you were in jail at the age of twelve?"

"Yes!" she said quickly.

"Did you really have a baby at the age of thirteen?"

"Yes!"

"Were you really homeless at the age of fifteen?"

"Oh, yes!"

"And even tried to kill yourself?"

"Yes!"

Looking into her beautiful, beaming face, I asked, "What or who turned your life around?"

"Well, a white Jewish lady by the name of Anne Cohn did. She looked at me and said, 'You know what? You have a million-dollar smile. And the world needs it. And guess what? I'm going to help bring that smile out of you.'"

Wow, what a Power Thought!

"How did she help you?"

"Well, Anne asked me, 'What do you want to be when you grow up?'

"I said, 'I'm all I can be. I made a mistake in life. I can't be anything else.'

"But she said to me, 'Your life is still in front of you. You're young. You can do anything you want to do. You just don't know what to do. But guess what? I know what to do and I can bring it out of you. I won't walk in front of you and I won't walk behind you. But I'm gonna walk beside you and catch you by the hand, and you and I can bring everything you want out of you, because it's there. You were born with it. You can be whatever you want to be.'"

"You believed it?" I asked Sweet Alice.

Alice smiled. "I believed it because I wanted to hear it. I had always heard that if you messed up, you couldn't do anything. This is it. I wanted to hear that I could be anything that I wanted to be. I wanted to hear I had a million-dollar smile. I don't know if I quite believed that, like I do now, but I needed to hear it. I needed somebody to say they cared. And because of that, I was willing to follow her and do whatever she wanted me to do."

"Sweet Alice," I went on, "that one Power Thought, 'Anybody can be somebody,' entered your mind at age fifteen and an amazing future was released for you. That was the beginning. When the Watts riots hit Los Angeles in 1965 you established a thing called 'POW.' Is that right?"

"That's right," she said, "POW—Parents of Watts! Just recently, someone called me from our local high school and said that the children down there were wearing T-shirts that said, 'Kill a cop.' We don't want anybody to be killed.

13

So I suggested, 'Let's go take those T-shirts off of them, find out who is making the shirts and get rid of them, because that's not what we want to have in our community.'

"I called the captain of the Police Department and I said to him, 'I need you to meet me in thirty minutes at the high school.'

"In thirty minutes he was down there. I said to him, 'Let's call the mayor and/or the governor and tell them that we don't want these T-shirts printed.'

"So guess what? We found out where they came from, and fired the man on the spot, closed up his business, and said to him, 'We don't want you in this community.'"

"Sweet Alice," I said, "I was in Johannesburg some weeks ago, and suddenly the CNN television in Johannesburg showed the black leaders talking about Los Angeles being burned down in '92. They complained that the government hasn't done anything for them. The governor didn't do anything. The President didn't do anything. And then, all of a sudden, you stood up and gave a terrific speech! What did you tell them?"

"I said, if anybody is going to do anything to help, God didn't give it to the government, He gave it to us! And we have to make the difference! The problem is, we want to sit back and blame somebody else. But we must make the difference."

Now there's a POWER THOUGHT!

"God gave us everything we needed when we were born. And if we don't use it, we lose it. Not the government, we have to do it. And the reason I know we have to do it is because I had already done it. As long as I sat back and waited on somebody else to start up a community program or give me some money, I didn't get it.

"So I took the house that I had been saving for a rainy day, gave it away, and started my own program in my own house. I gave my house to the homeless and the poor. I said they could have it. And guess what? Out of giving away that one house, God has added nine more houses, because the more you give to God, the more He gives back. It belongs to Him."

You are destined to be a part of this wonderful community of human beings called Power Thinkers.

How do I know you well enough to make that impertinent prediction? Well, you bought this book. Or someone gave it to you. At least you are reading this sentence. That means you are the kind of person who is attracted to the message of this book. You are a potential Power Thinker!

2

What Is
Power Thinking?

Positive Thinking? Possibility Thinking? Power Thinking?

Positive Thinking? ——That's Faith.

Possibility Thinking? —That's Faith that is focused.

Power Thinking? ———That's Focused Faith filled with
Following-Through Power.

Faith + Focus + Follow-Through = SUCCESS

Positive Thinking entered the vocabulary and the consciousness of human beings in the middle of this twentieth century.

What is it?

16

Why was it accepted?

And why was it rejected by others?

We'll see as these pages unfold.

Let me tell you how I was introduced to the person who was the founder of "positive thinking." His name: Norman Vincent Peale.

I had completed Hope College in Holland, Michigan, a leading, fully accredited liberal arts institution. I was a student for four years, 1943–1947. I was taught to be a critical thinker. I majored in history. And gave serious time and attention to sociology and psychology. Upon graduation with a bachelor of arts degree I was accepted in a postgraduate school for studies in theology. In three years I would be prepared for my lifetime as a professional clergyman. The denomination that I belonged to was the oldest Protestant denomination with a continuous and unbroken ministry in the United States—the Dutch Reformed Church in America.

We were proud that fifty-four Dutch colonists bought Manhattan Island from the Indians in 1628 and founded New Amsterdam. Later it would become a part of the British empire and be renamed New York. We would be 148 years old by the time 1776 rolled around and a new country was organized called the United States of America.

For over three hundred years this denomination had established careful guidelines for the morality, the education, and the self-discipline of men who would be eligible for ordination as ministers in the church.

Norman Vincent Peale was the pastor of our original church: the Marble Collegiate Church of New York. By the time I was a seminary student he was famous. One night the

students were told that he was speaking at a public appearance at the civic center in Grand Rapids, Michigan. None of us had ever heard him speak. Since he was so famous, a carload of us went from the seminary to the civic center to hear this great minister.

At that point I had spent four years listening to speakers every day at Hope College. They were professors. And I listened to speakers every day at Western Theological Seminary. They were all professors. The greatest people that I knew were my professors. They were so profound, so professorial in their personality and in their articulation. They were very rational, very cognitive, and so nonemotional, lacking in the kind of excitement and enthusiasm that marks the simple person on the street, and in the sales offices of the world.

I had lived in this different world of academia year after year after year for over five years. I was not prepared for Norman Vincent Peale.

The civic center was crowded. It was packed. He made his appearance on stage and was warmly applauded.

Then he opened his mouth.

He began to speak.

His vocabulary was very nonintellectual. The words he used were all simple words, like a high school or a grade school teacher.

He made no profound, provocative statements. He was not boring. He was very emotional. That reading was picked up by my heart and my head and caused me to be less than respectful. He did not come across as very intellectual. Surely he was not the kind of "speaker" I was used to in the classrooms of academia. The truth is he told a few stories. The audience loved him. They hung on his very word. They roared with laughter and upon occasion I could see hands reach upward as if to dry away tears from an eye.

I went home with my roommates in the car and we all agreed that he was "Simple. Shallow. Emotional. And didn't really have 'much to say.'" "We had nothing to learn from him."

How wrong I was. I had an awful lot to learn from him. But I didn't realize it.

Only a couple of years later I would complete my graduate work. And I would receive a special degree for my thesis, which was done over a three-year period under faculty supervision. It was a major project entitled "A Topical Index to the *Institutes of the Christian Religion*" of John Calvin, a brilliant French lawyer. To complete that project in three years required that I read every word ten times in all four historical, theological volumes. I read all four books at least ten times.

It was one of the most profound and personally challenging reading assignments that I ever chose. My work added up to over two hundred pages and was enthusiastically approved by the faculty. And a copy bound in leather still remains to this day at the Western Theological Seminary in Holland, Michigan.

Then I graduated.

I passed all of my tests.

I was learned.

I was educated.

I was an intellectual.

My academic degrees became my number-one ego trip.

Positive thinking? Norman Vincent Peale? I had turned that off long ago.

I became the pastor of a little Reformed church in Chicago, Illinois. There were thirty-seven members, ninteen against eighteen.

I walked right into a conflicting, divided, fighting church. It was terrible.

I didn't know what I was getting into.

I didn't want to take sides. It was a new church. The founding pastor was controversial. And by the slightest majority the members voted to expel him. Now I stepped into the remnant.

Eighteen people were hurt that their founding pastor had been fired. Nineteen people were thrilled that they "won."

It was a social, spiritual, psychological mess.

I prayed. And the wisdom I got gave me the message to "Forget about these thirty-seven people. Try to personally deal with each person's hurts as positively as you can. Meanwhile go out and ring doorbells, win new members, and overpower them with a new mass immigration of healthy, happy people."

That is precisely what I did.

I began to ring doorbells.

"Are you an active member of a local church?" I would ask. And if the answer was negative I would get excited and enthused and say "Well, I'm in a new church here and I need you. I think I can help you and I think you can help me."

They laughed and so did I.

At about that same time I somehow got on the mailing list of Norman Vincent Peale. Every month I would receive copies of his sermons preached to the Marble Collegiate Church. I would always read the title—the cover of the little booklet. Then I would skim through the contents.

Almost always I saw nothing but a couple of stories and it didn't have enough of those profound, abstract statements in the deep Calvinistic theological category that this brain had been working in for three years absorbing the greatest theological textbooks ever written.

So I threw the cheap little printed Peale sermons away.

But unintentionally, and unknowingly, my subconscious made a mental recording of the titles of these Peale sermons. Titles like, "Trouble Doesn't Need to Trouble You." Or "How to Make Your Dreams Come True." Or "Positive Thinking Can Change You for the Better."

These titles were simple. Aimed at meeting a deep emotional human need. Now, without my approval, they entered and remained recorded in my memory system!

<u>Power thoughts</u>, silently, seductively entered this proud, young, educated minister's subconscious where they would quietly wait in the stillness of that creative center. I didn't even know they were there and that they would one day appear when I would need the kind of desperate help only they could deliver.

Help—called "Hope."

Emotional osmosis was happening without my knowledge, approval, or awareness. Amazingly, miraculously, my internalized subconscious was being changed.

21

I became internally changed by all of these dozens and dozens and dozens of sentences that were titles to the Peale sermons.

I became a positive thinker.

Even though I could not have defined that if a professor asked me to define it. I had never taken a course in all of my classes in psychology, or in all of my studies of theology, defining positive thinking versus negative thinking.

I became a positive-thinking person.

Forty years later I would define positive thinking as "faith." That's about all that it is. And that's almost everything! "Faith" is a biblical word. "Faith" is a religious word. While "positive thinking" defines the same essential human behavior in words that are secularized and not soaked with religiosity.

Norman Vincent Peale didn't know it. But he turned me from a "negative thinker" to a "positive thinker."

And that would become Possibility Thinking.

After reading the Norman Vincent Peale sermons for a few years I now found myself called by the denomination to begin a new church on the Pacific Coast. My salary of two hundred dollars a month was guaranteed by the sponsoring denomination. That was headed by a board of persons from throughout the nation. The chairman of that board was Ruth Stafford Peale, the wife of Norman Vincent Peale. With that guarantee I moved to California with my wife as the only member, and with five hundred dollars as a donation from the denomination, I was given the freedom to dream dreams and to build a new church from scratch.

I was convinced I had a powerful message to share with

people who had no religion and never went to church. And these were the people with whom I wanted to share my positive faith. I didn't want to "convert" them. I only wanted to "help" them. And my optimism and my positive emotional feelings on a daily basis were so meaningful in my life that I wanted to share this kind of a "philosophy" or "faith" or "relationship with Christ" with people who had never experienced living this way.

So I simply wanted to build a great church and made a forty-year commitment to do so. Literally, and honestly, I thought it might take a forty-year commitment to succeed. After all, the Marble Collegiate Church with Norman Vincent Peale was well over three hundred years old!

If I could take my one lifetime, spend it in one place, continually building this new church a little better and bigger and nicer year after year after year, then certainly after forty years I ought to be able to have a great church and leave something beautiful for a new world to enjoy.

It was at that time that the words of Jesus entered my mind and the words were:

"If you have faith as small as a mustard seed, you can say to this mountain, 'Move from here to there' and it will move. Nothing will be impossible for you."

(Matthew 17:20)

• I became a Possibility Thinker!

I began to focus my power of positive thinking to discover my personal potential and then go on to discover possible ways to achieve a seemingly impossible objective.

23

I dreamed of ten possible places that I could conceivably use to share my messages and start a church. I thought of all the possible ways of building <u>something out of nothing</u>.

I have lived for nearly forty years with that. I called and still call it "Possibility Thinking." <u>That's faith focused on achieving a definite goal</u>.

I have since said some people fail because they lack faith. Others fail because they fail to focus, and others fail because they fail to follow through day after day after day.

Certainly nothing significant ever happens until a person has the vision, and the faith.

Positive thinking is the faith that gets you into a mental climate where you begin to imagine what you might become or what you might achieve. Years later I would "preach a sermon" on what I was beginning to live out and experience.

- Faith stimulates success.
- Hope sustains success.
- Love sanctifies success.

Faith gets success started, but focus is what gives the vision its cutting edge. Some people have the faith, but fail simply because they haven't "<u>focused</u>" on a measurable, manageable, meaningful objective.

Many people with a positive-thinking attitude have the capacity to imagine such a wide variety of visions and dreams that they are easily distracted from focusing on their one single most important passion and purpose: their God-given calling.

When you take a magnifying glass, and allow the sun

24

to send its rays magnified through the glass in your hand until it becomes a tiny, burning sun on a leaf or a piece of paper— only then can you watch the fire start and the smoke come up off the dry paper or leaf.

<u>Positive Thinking</u> is faith.

<u>Possibility Thinking</u> is faith that is Focused!

<u>Power Thinking</u> is a focused faith that consistently and persistently follows the plan through in detail to completion. For Power Thinkers realize that *failure follows those who fail to follow through.*

Yes,

FAITH + FOCUS + FOLLOW-THROUGH = SUCCESS.

Therefore,

Positive Thinking + Possibility Thinking + Power Thinking = <u>Success!</u>

For the last half of this twentieth century we have been hit with Positive Thinking: Positive mental attitude: Possibility Thinking: Success and motivation.

At the end of this century evidence mounts in favor of this mental wave length called "the positive approach."

A. The late Dr. Norman Cousins reported that when brains are stimulated with a positive thought the brain secretes chemicals. We all know that glandular secretions are stimulated by ideas. Sweat glands, sex glands we understand. Now we know the brain likewise secretes healing chemicals called endorphins! Power Thoughts—Welcome!

B. Dr. David Burns is the founder of the newest and perhaps most exciting theory of psychology called "cognitive

therapy." In essence it establishes conclusively that positive thoughts can be harnessed to feed the brain healthy stimulations energizing the human personality. Call these ideas <u>Power Thoughts</u>.

C. Self-esteem psychology has finally found its place. Nearly twenty-five years ago I published the book, *Self-Love— The Dynamic Force of Success*. I followed that with another, *Self-Esteem—The New Reformation*. W. Clement Stone felt that message was so seminal he purchased 250,000 copies and mailed one to every pastor in the United States, Catholic and Protestant. Criticism was not withheld. But self-esteem is now recognized along with "self-worth," "self-respect" and "human dignity" as the ultimate human value that cannot be compromised.

I have heard, listened and evaluated the criticism leveled at "Positive Thinking," "Possibility Thinking," "Success Philosophy" and "Self-Esteem Psychology."

Many of the arguments must be understood. Some of the criticism is deserved. But we cannot and must not allow wise negative criticisms to allow the baby to be thrown out with the dirty water.

Even as we acknowledge the newly discovered power of the positive approaches, we must also face the criticisms that may linger.

POWER? CONTROL? OWNERSHIP?

Before I share the substance and the strategy of Power Thinking, let me share what's most important and that's the spirit that must drive Power Thinking.

POWER THINKING
IT IS NOT A SELFISH SPIRIT OF "CONTROL"—
OR "POWER" OR "OWNERSHIP"!

CONTROL
POWER THINKING DOES SEEK CONTROL—
BUT NOT OPPRESSIVE POWER.

CONTROL IS NOT DESIRED TO MANIPULATE, INTIMIDATE
OR OPPRESS.

But control is essential if and when we must stand accountable and be personally responsible for our behavior.

So control is sought to minimize waste, maximize productivity, and fulfill personal responsibility, accepting personal accountability. That's called creative management in a noncollectivistic system.

OWNERSHIP
POWER THINKING SEEKS OWNERSHIP,
BUT NOT EXPLOITATION.

Ownership is solicited and sought to maximize our opportunities in personal freedom to share and give our talents and skills in creative community adventures.

POWER
Now then catch the positive, healing, inspiring, redeeming spirit of Power Thinking. This spirit will protect you and immunize you from the dangers inherent in the system.

THE SPIRIT OF POWER THINKING.

Power Thinking is not **arrogant thinking—it is self-confident thinking.** It is aware that it does not know all of the answers and that there are other people who are brighter, more knowledgeable, better connected and more up to date in advanced knowledge. It has the self-confidence to believe that it can be a part of really making a difference in the world.

One of the greatest Power Thoughts to affect me was the statement of Louis I. Kahn, the great architect, who said, "If I've got all the answers when I'm ready to start a project, I can be sure of this: SOME OF MY ANSWERS ARE WRONG!"

Arrogance—"Know-It-All"—is not a part of Power Thinking. Power Thinking is ready and willing to change its mind, and alter its course in the face of reality.

<u>It is reality thinking</u>, <u>even while opening its imaginations to the power of creative fantasizing</u>.

Power Thinking is rooted in integrity, humble enough to confront reality honestly, and make swift, smart and sensible changes.

The Queen of England's private yacht was cruising through the Mediterranean. Captain Smith was invited to have an evening dinner with Her Majesty. The dining room was exquisite in its elegant setting: the linen cloth on the table, the monogrammed linen napkins, the fresh-cut flowers in the centerpiece, the Irish crystal, the sterling silver—it was beautiful!

The pleasures to the lip, the eye, the ear and the

28

tongue were delightful. As the candles burned down, the captain touched his lips with his napkin and folded it gently on the table. He looked across at his royal hostess and said, "Your Majesty, if you would please excuse me I must return to the bridge to make sure things are in good order for the night of cruising."

"Of course, Captain. It's been wonderful dining with you. Please be excused."

As the captain left the dining room and approached the steps that led to the bridge, he relished his personal pride. It was the emotional dessert that his heart was feasting on right now.

Yes, he was proud of who he was.

And the ship that he commanded.

And the respect he earned from the Queen herself.

As he reached the top of the steps he was able to see at the wheel two uniformed officers who were at his command in charge on the bridge. In front of them the long window enabled the captain at the helm to be able to see to the right, to the left and to the horizon. Just as the captain reached the bridge he was jolted by a light in the path ahead. The light was bright enough to suggest that this was a sizable cruise ship. "Send them a command to 'alter your course,'" the captain ordered his signal master.

Instantly the signal master flashed this message to the fast approaching light.

Now the three uniformed officers on the Queen's vessel stood straight. Waiting.

The approaching light flashed the answer, "You alter your course."

Captain Smith was indignant. "Tell them who we are. Give them my name. Tell them this is Her Majesty's private vessel and the Queen is aboard. And repeat the order 'you alter your course.'"

The signal master sent out the message: "My name is Captain Russell Smith. This is Her Royal Majesty's private yacht. The Queen is aboard. This is a Royal Command. You will alter your course."

They waited. For what seemed like minutes there was no answer. Then the approaching light responded. This was his message: "My name is Tom Johnson. I've been in charge of this lighthouse for sixteen years. **You will alter YOUR course.**"

The spirit of Power Thinking? It is self-confident, but not arrogant. It is loyal and deeply committed, but it knows when and where and how to change in the face of reality. The spirit of Power Thinking is smart and humble enough to admit without embarrassment, "You were right! I was wrong! Thank you!"

POWER THINKING is caring : **not self-centered, self-seeking, self-serving, self-aggrandizing.** It lives by an "illuminated self-interest." Power Thinkers intuitively, instinctively or intelligently become aware that they are going to bring happiness to themselves only as they genuinely bring encouragement to other people.

I saw a story on the Cable News Network. The story was about an elderly woman. She was eighty-six years old. She had been in a coma in the hospital for months. Finally, her family and her doctor decided to take her off the life-support systems. As they got ready to disconnect the system which provided nourishment to her body, one young doctor stopped them. "Pulling the plug is a very dangerous thing to do," he said. As he spoke he reached over and started to stroke the ailing woman's arm with loving, warm strokes.

Within a short time the old woman opened her eyes. It was an incredible thing to witness. The old woman looked up at the doctor with her beautiful, clear eyes and said, "I didn't think anyone cared."

Who were the real power thinkers? The persons who made what they felt was the intelligent decision to "pull the plug," or the young doctor who exercised the ultimate act: "tender touching"?

POWER THINKING is not naïve. Certainly—it is constructively critical. To simply say "everything's going to be fantastic" and to deny looking at the practical realities is not smart. And Power Thinking will not have real power long if it isn't smart.

Recently I watched an interview on television. I was attracted because a member of the board of directors of Robert Schuller's ministry in Europe was on the screen. His name is Andreas Van Agt. He is the ambassador from the European Community to the United States of America. He is a dear friend, a great supporter and a wise counselor. The cameras cut from him to a circle of five prominent persons discussing global finance.

One of these persons was Lord Carrington. He made the comment:

"Well, the problem between France and England is

quite simple. The French are conceptual. We British are pragmatic."

The truth is, I thought to myself, that does not mean that the two need necessarily be either competitive or contradictory. They can be mutually complementary!

I am a conceptual person. My wife of well over forty years is pragmatic. I get the dreams and ideas. She instantly perceives the challenges, the problems and the difficulties involved in the proposal. She is pragmatic. I am conceptual. <u>But Power Thinkers see the conceptual and the pragmatic as complementary—not conflicting.</u>

Because my wife sees the potential problems, obstacles and difficulties, and I see fantastic possibilities, we simply join hearts and heads in a paradigm to <u>strategize success</u>. So we approach our commitment to a great dream knowing that one of the positive things we must do is "prepare" <u>to prevent encountering the most obvious possible difficulties</u>. We must manage the unfolding Power Thoughts without aborting the positive potential in the proposal. We wisely strategize how to develop this beautiful dream by neutralizing or negating the negative potential while we exploit the positive potential.

So Power Thinkers are constructively critical. They ask tough questions.

• What's the competition, if any?

• What inherent contradictions need to be recognized and dealt with?

• What compromises will I have to make?

Power Thinkers are not afraid of contradictions. I learned years ago that I probably am denying the reality of a truth until I dare to step forward and enter into the space that separates contradictions.

Power Thinking sees contradictions as challenging opportunities to be creative in compromising. So the fabric designer picks contrasting and contradictory colors, puts them together in the same fabric and comes up with something very exciting. "Look how she uses the yellows, the oranges, the purples and the reds together!"

The composer of great music does the same thing. Minor chords clash and contradict with other minor chords until they set the stage for a dramatic, positive conclusion in marvelous major chords.

It's true in architecture, in music, in art, and it's true in theology, too. Justice demands that bad people be punished. Mercy demands that they be forgiven. In the positive Christian faith this is the ultimate contradiction. It's why Christians around the world for 2,000 years have put a cross at the top of their steeples, or on their altars, remembering how Jesus Christ died. Christians believe that the Cross is the creative reminder that God was able to solve the contradiction between justice and mercy by offering forgiveness. Forgiveness was "purchased by Christ" in his "dying on the cross" or "taking the rap for me," as a young Christian teenager recently put it.

POWER THINKING is not Pollyanna thinking—it dares to face problems.

That's why Power Thinkers become maximum achievers. This is an extension of the fact that they are not naïve, but they are wisely and wonderfully critical. A naïve,

33

Pollyanna person who will believe any preposterous proposition offered by a super zealot is a weak thinker, not a Power Thinker, if he sets aside the critical part of his mental capabilities.

To spot a shortfall, to observe a weakness, to perceive a problem, is not "negative thinking." Power thinking welcomes the wisdom that comes with noticing problems that exist or problems that are bound to be confronted without wise planning that could make possible the prevention of problems.

When God created the human brain it was with the capacity to be constructively critical. Note the real difference between a negative-thinking critic and a positive-thinking critic.

Negative thinking aborts power thoughts because it see something wrong with the proposal. Positive power thinking expects to see difficulties, challenges, problems, imperfections, shortfalls. But it believes that the positive potential can be safely isolated, immunized, and then developed constructively, profitably, creatively, redemptively.

That's why positive Power Thinkers ultimately emerge as the real achievers.

I have friends in North Dakota who are big potato farmers. They tell the story of a potato farmer who moved from Idaho to North Dakota.

He bought a big potato farm from a retiring Dakota farmer. He let everybody know that he himself knew "how to raise potatoes, because we've been in that business in Idaho for a long time."

The local farmers noticed, out of the corners of their eyes, that the "foreigner" from Idaho bought good seed potatoes, and planted them at the same time and style as they did. They also quietly observed that he knew how to cultivate the sprouting fields. And even used the same machinery to harvest the potatoes, digging them out of the ground onto a wagon pulled behind.

But then they observed a difference. He took the wagonload of potatoes right out of the ground and hauled them directly to town. He didn't separate or sort them.

Well, all of the North Dakota farmers sold their potatoes at the same place. It was a co-op. And the arrangement for years and years was quite simple. The co-op paid a top price for potatoes if they were sorted when they were brought in and unloaded. Always the potatoes were a mixture of big ones, medium ones and little ones as they came out of the ground. So upon harvesting they were dumped from the wagon onto the ground, to be hand-separated by size into one of three piles: Big potatoes pile. Medium potatoes pile. Small potatoes pile.

The farmers were all aware of the fact that if they took the time to empty the potatoes on the ground, hand-separate them, and then deliver them to town so they could be unloaded according to their size, then they would receive maximum dollars. That was what the wise North Dakota farmers had been doing for years.

But not this new fellow from Idaho. So everyone knew that he was either very rich and didn't need maximum dollar return, or he was very foolish or lazy.

One of the old Dakota farmers happened to be at the co-op when he watched the manager—a longtime friend in the community—hand a check to the Idaho farmer. He couldn't help but make a shocking observation.

The Idaho farmer was paid the same amount of money, even though he brought the potatoes in right out of the field without separating them by size. The Idaho farmer took his check. With a "thanks a lot," he excused himself and left. The North Dakota farmer looked at his old friend, the manager of the co-op, and said: "I couldn't help but notice. He got the same price as all the rest of us. But we all separate our potatoes so that when they are unloaded the big potatoes go in the big section, the medium potatoes go in the medium section, the little potatoes go in the little section. That's a lot of work on our part. You paid him the same amount and he never separated them. I can't believe it."

"Oh, but John, you're wrong," the co-op manager answered. "When he unloaded the potatoes, he unloaded all of his big potatoes in the big bin, and his medium potatoes in the medium bin, and his little potatoes in the little bin. When he brought his wagonload of potatoes here they were all separated. The little potatoes were all at the bottom, the medium size were all in the middle and the big potatoes were all at the top." The old, well-experienced Dakota potato farmer shook his head in disbelief.

The co-op manager continued: "But, John, you know the difference? You all take the nice road into town. He took the country roads with holes and bumps! And, John, <u>big potatoes always rise to the top on a rough road</u>."

Power Thinkers are empowered by problems. They're "successed out"—not "stressed out"—by challenges. They exercise positive reality thinking.

• "I created these problems for myself."
• "I made decisions that caused me to be where I am today. That's why I'm facing the challenge."
• "So I have nobody to blame but myself."
• "That means that I'll not be angry, or cynical, or suspicious."
• "I'll assume responsibility for these problems."
• "I got myself into it—I can get myself out of it."
• "I still believe that every obstacle is an opportunity: To learn. To grow. To be corrected or protected from making mistakes. So all of this is good news!"
• "So I'm not discouraged—I'm motivated by this new challenge."
• "I'm not depressed—I'm impressed."

No wonder BIG POTATOES RISE TO THE TOP ON A ROUGH ROAD!

Yes, Power Thinking believes that every problem has a solution somewhere that can match it.

<u>Every mountain can be moved</u>. It may not go away, but I may change my perspective of the mountain as an obstacle and begin to spot it as an opportunity. I can begin to see it as something that holds greater minerals waiting to be mined and exploited. And if my perception of a problem sees it diminished in its negative intensity, and if my new paradigm of the problem is shifted until it becomes a possibility, then indeed the mountain has moved in my mind! It moved

from a negative to a positive! Which is one reason why Jesus was teaching a profound truth when He said, "If you have faith as small as a mustard seed, you can say to this mountain, 'Move from here to there' and it will move. Nothing will be impossible for you." (Matthew 17:20)

Yes, Power Thinkers are problem facers. Problem chasers, problem erasers. They literally welcome problems and turn them into possibilities.

POWER THINKING IS not narrow-minded—it is broad-minded.

It has learned to think big enough for God to fit in.

The hardest job in the world is thinking bigger than you've ever thought before.

Yesterday I called on a man who has been a very close friend of mine for nearly thirty years. While I was building my church, he was building his business. I started from scratch. So did he. I would speak for him and he would speak for me. Today he is a multi-billionaire and I challenged him to think bigger. I said, "It's like the old story I've always told about the fisherman and his frying pan. Right?" And he answered, "I don't know the story." I couldn't imagine that. We'd shared so many platforms together. And I've told the story a hundred times around the world in Japan, Hong Kong, Korea, Russia, Germany, Sweden, and many other countries. When they translate it into the different languages, the audience response is an experience to remember.

"Tell me the story, Bob." And I did.

"There was a tourist who walked by the ocean and saw an old man sitting on the pier with a fishing pole. At his side was a large bucket where he could take his catch home. Next to it was a wooden ruler that had been broken off at the ten-inch mark.

"The tourist watched the old man's pole bend, watched him pull in a fish, watched him hold on to the slippery, twisting little creature, and with his broken ruler he measured his catch. It was about seven inches long. He took it off the hook and put it in the bucket. He'd have supper tonight. The next catch: same size. Into the bucket, and so it went. Suddenly the pole bent hard and heavy. And it was a much larger fish. The old man was able to hold on to the fighting, squirming, twisting, slippery, strong fish while he measured it and it was well over the ten-inch ruler in length. Probably twelve or thirteen inches long. He maneuvered the hook out of the mouth and instead of throwing this prize catch into his bucket, he threw it back into the ocean. The tourist was really perplexed and said, 'Why do you keep the little fish and throw the big one away?'

"The old man looked around, blinked, and said: 'See this ruler? It's a ten-inch ruler. I had it broken off at the ten-inch mark because I have to measure the fish. If they are bigger than ten inches, I throw them back in. If they're under ten inches I keep them. I keep the little ones and I throw the big ones away because <u>my frying pan is only ten inches wide.</u> '"

My friend laughed. And I said to him (calling him by his first name), "That's true for me. And it's also true for you. Both of us are successful. But both of us have thrown the biggest fish back. The biggest ideas that came into my mind I didn't take seriously. Neither have you." He looked ready to challenge me, and I said: "You never did announce that you'd be available as a candidate for President of the United States." Our eyes locked. I was telling the truth. He'd considered it for a while, but no, he never made <u>that commitment</u>. And he could have made a great President.

"So we have to think bigger," I said to him. He agreed. The truth is that both of us have received a large measure of achievement only because we have been basically capable of thinking bigger again and again and again.

Power-thinking people are people who have learned the art of careful, and dareful, and prayerful compromising.

Narrow-minded thinkers are tempted to continually narrow their definitions, and their interpretations.

"Exclusivity," not "inclusivity," characterizes the negative small thinkers. They can become so elitist that they diminish the network of the supporters that really would love to help them, cater to them, promote them or support them.

Power Thinkers think globally, transculturally, transreligiously, transracially. As we shall see, they think "<u>Coalition—not Collision</u>"; they move from competition to cooperation.

The Power Thinkers of tomorrow will be broad-minded people.

This does not mean that they will not have their own definite set of personal standards and beliefs that they will hold to openly, honestly and forthrightly.

But they will have learned how to be <u>friendly</u>, <u>fair</u>, <u>frank</u> and <u>firm</u>.

And that's diplomacy at its best. That's the spirit of power-thinking achievers of today and, more than ever, tomorrow.

Power Thinking is acting as if we are what we wish we were:

Dr. David Meyer, head of the Psychology Department at Hope College, my alma mater in Holland, Michigan, is the author of the single most widely used textbook on psychology chosen by colleges and universities in America. His latest book, *The Pursuit of Happiness,* gives this wise counsel: "You want to be happy? Smile! And keep smiling."

Smiling is good, healthy exercise.

Smiling is a sign of health.

Smiling is the universal sign of happiness.

Smiling is using a divinely designed possibility guaranteed to give you an instant uplift.

Dr. Meyer continued, "Try some fun little experiments that manipulate your facial expressions as instruments."

"Turn up the corner of your mouth, please.

"Now the other corner.

"Now raise the cheeks."

Dr. Meyer also shares this exciting new finding in psychological research. "People find cartoons funnier and they feel better when they're suddenly manipulated into a smile," he reports, adding, "It even happens, by the way, that if people will bite on a pen, which activates one of the smiling muscles, they find cartoons funnier."

Power Thinkers believe that <u>if we will begin acting as if we are what we would like to be, we will begin to generate the positive emotions that we would normally experience if and when our desires were really fulfilled.</u>

Going through the motions can give premature birth to the positive emotions!

41

Here's a very simple but powerful principle: <u>We are as likely to act ourselves into a way of thinking and feeling as we are to feel ourselves into a new way of acting.</u>

And so if we want to change ourselves in some important way, we ought not to just sit on our duffs waiting for inspiration to strike us. We need to get up and start acting the way we would want to be. Go through the motions of happiness, if that's how we want to feel.

Dr. Meyer also contends: The evidence is consistent concerning the link <u>between people's experience of faith and their experience of joy.</u> C. S. Lewis once said, "Joy is the serious business of Heaven." And there's a lot of evidence now to confirm this.

We have new evidence that people of faith live happier lives period. In surveys done by George Gallup, people who say they are highly spiritually committed and believe that their faith is very important to them are emotionally healthier people. They pray regularly. These people are <u>twice</u> as likely to say they are very happy as people whom Gallup scores as low in spiritual commitment.

Also, there are new studies on how people cope with crises such as bereavement, disability, unemployment or divorce. And, in each of these areas, studies have found that people cope better if they are strengthened by an inner faith!

"Faith seems to serve what sociologists call a buffering effect. It doesn't take the tragedy out of the traumatic event, but it enables people more easily to recover a sense of joy," is Dr. Meyer's latest report.

What Dr. Meyer has articulated and what the experts have studied I, too, have experienced.

People often ask me, "You smile all the time. Are you always happy?" And I say, "Not always, but I have to lift people up—so I think a smile will do more than a frown." But, believe it or not, after I smiled, even when I did not feel like smiling, I felt like smiling after I had smiled.

SMILE—ANYWAY!
SMILE—EVERY DAY!
SMILE ALL THE WAY!

<u>Power Thinking is acting like we are what we would like to be!</u> It sees the fun, the humor in life.
That's Power Thinking!
It's not an electronic process.
It's not a digital process.
It's not a laser process.
It is a far more complex, creative, powerful spiritual process.
And guess what?
You have it in you!
Let's find it!
And follow it!
This is going to be fun!

3

The Creative Process of Power Thinking

What's the difference between humans and the other animals that rank intellectually highest in the animal kingdom? Some theorists have suggested that the difference is that man is a laughing creature! We humans are unique in our capacity to sense and structure humor. Laughter is certainly part of the human spirit and it allows our secret creativity to be released. No animal matches the human being in creativity—and humor sets the stage. What a divine design we are!

Carlyle didn't agree that man is the only laughing creature. "There are the laughing hyenas," he said. Wrong, Carlyle! Child and adult psychologists agree: Animals don't laugh. Laughter—that happy sound—is the audio eruption that is rooted in deep emotion. It is distinctly an expression of the human spirit.

Watkins's contribution to this discussion is really exciting. "Humans," he reported, "are the only creatures that can <u>learn,</u>" When a lark sings its first melody, it is already perfect. The bird does not improve the melody. When the spider spins its web for the first time, it will never do it any better. When the bee first creates its delicious honey, it will never improve the process.

Animals can be trained to do certain things, but they cannot cognitively improve the process. They do not <u>learn</u> in the sense of "evaluating," "measuring" and "grading" their performances, then intentionally move to a higher level of creativity—<u>deciding to make things better</u>.

You and all other human beings are

> conceptualized,
> designed,
> engineered,
> invented,
> conceived,
> created
> and empowered

to be the world's only creatures that are:

"POWER THOUGHT PROCESSORS."

I don't care who you are, where you come from, what race or religion you may be, what your level of education or economics, culture, skill or talent is—

YOU HAVE GREAT POTENTIAL!

You haven't yet discovered your ultimate potential.

So—don't rob from the next generation by withholding from them what you could conceivably achieve. We should rush to welcome the good news that we can do more, be more, have more, give more. Why don't we?

One reason why we fail to scale the peak of our personal potential is negative programming!

Many of us are incapable of realizing our potential merely because someone else has given us a negative impression of who we are, what we can be or what we can accomplish. To discover your potential, reject the negative programming all of us are exposed to.

I was recently asked, "Dr. Schuller, of all the people you've interviewed, who is the most impressive person you've ever met?"

"Well," I replied, "I don't know if I can answer that."

They kept pressing me, and one name kept coming to my mind. I said, "Probably George Dantzig."

"I never heard of him," they said.

"Well," I replied, "it's an amazing story. Let me tell it to you." This was the story:

I was on my way home from Europe. I had boarded a nonstop flight from New York to Los Angeles. The man seated next to me said nothing, I remained quiet also. So I opened my briefcase to study. It was a Saturday, and I had to prepare my message for the next morning in my church. In my open briefcase was one of my books with my picture on the back cover. My seatmate saw the picture. He looked at me, and put two and two together.

"You write books?"

"Yes, I do."

"What about?"

"Oh, many things. One of my favorite topics is 'Possibility Thinking.'"

"That's interesting, I write books, too."

"What about?"

"Mathematics."

"Oh!" I said. I didn't tell him I got a D in mathematics at Hope College. Now here I was sitting next to a mathematics author! Suddenly I was hit by a new thought.

"You know, I have always believed that Positive Thinking and Possibility Thinking apply to all areas of life, but for the first time in my life, I realize they don't have any bearing when it comes to mathematics, do they? I mean, five plus five equals ten, whether you're a negative thinker or a positive thinker, right?"

He looked at me and he said, "Dr. Schuller, that's not true. My name is George Dantzig. Do you know who I am?"

"No."

"Well, I'm returning from Vienna, where the President of the United States appointed me to the International Higher Mathematics Committee."

"Oh."

"Now, let me tell you my story. Nearly fifty years ago I was a mathematics student at the University of California at Berkeley. It was a week before graduation. This was during the Depression and people were standing in lines to get soup. They were hungry. All of us who were graduating were anticipating joining the unemployment line, for jobs were scarce. The rumor was, however, that the person who got the highest

marks in my class would be given a job as an assistant teacher.

"Now," he continued, "I was desperate. I did not want to stand in a soup line. I worked and worked and studied and prepared for the final exam. In fact, I studied so hard that when I went to take the test, I was late. I ran to the desk, picked up the paper and looked at it. It had eight problems. I solved all eight. Then I noticed there were two more that were written on the board. I tried the first and I couldn't get that one, so I switched to the other. I couldn't solve that one either. I went back to the first. The bell rang. I said to the professor, 'There are a couple of problems I didn't get finished. May I have a little more time?' He said, 'Sure, George. You have until Friday, at four o'clock, no later. Put it on my desk when you're done.' And I said, 'Okay, sir. I will.'

"I went home and I knew, I <u>knew</u> that there were students in my class who were as smart as I was. Some of them would have all ten problems solved. I was stuck on two of them, but I knew that <u>somebody</u> would solve those two. Why not <u>me</u>? I was as smart as they were. I worked on one of the problems. Couldn't solve it. Went to the other one. Couldn't solve it. Day after day, night after night, Tuesday night. Wednesday night. Thursday. Finally, I solved one, then the other. I put the paper on my professor's desk at four o'clock Friday. He wasn't there, so I just left it and I walked away, feeling very unsure of my future.

"Sunday morning, Dr. Schuller, about seven o'clock, there was a loud pounding on my door. I woke up, opened the door, groggily. There was my professor.

48

"He said, 'George! George! You made mathematics history.' I shook my head and said, 'What do you mean?'

"He said, 'George, I was thinking as I came over here. You came to class late for the test, didn't you?' I said, 'Yes. I'm sorry.'

"He said, 'No, no, no. It's okay. Eight problems were on the test paper that you picked up off my desk. You solved them all correctly. The two problems I had written on the board were <u>not</u> a part of the test! George, when I handed out the test, I said, 'I've enjoyed teaching all of you these four years. The rest of your life, if you want to have a little fun with mathematics—keep playing with these two famous unsolved problems.' Then I put those two problems on the blackboard. Even Einstein, to his death, played with those problems and couldn't solve them. <u>You</u> solved them, George! <u>You</u> solved them <u>both</u>! And I'm here to tell you—you've got a job, starting next week as my assistant professor!'"

George Dantzig looked at me and said, "Dr. Schuller, if I hadn't been late for that class, and if I had heard the professor say that these two problems remain unsolved, that even Einstein couldn't solve them, then do you think I would have believed that I could solve them? I wouldn't even have <u>tried</u> to solve them!"

Now here's the message! You have more potential to create, communicate and relate than you have been told. You have been mentally programmed to believe in the impossible! Maybe that was true before, <u>but not anymore</u>! New people, new powers, new hi-tech possibilities, have turned impossibilities into possibilities! Clear out and clean out that negative

programming and incredible potential will be released within you. Negative programming can hold us back from discovering and developing our potential. So can the Jonah Complex.

Abraham Maslow, one of the great psychologists of this century and creator of "Actualization Psychology," raised, as I do, this all-important question: "Why do humans virtually run from their gift to potentialize?" Maslow theorized that everybody would like to be better than they are. We all have within us an impulse to improve ourselves, an impulse toward actualizing our possibilities. Then what holds us back? Maslow said we are blocked by a restraining force he called "the Jonah Complex." Just as Jonah ran away from God, turning his back on the great possibilities that God had lined up for him, so we fear our own greatness; we evade our higher destiny; we deliberately choose to run away from our best talents. We fear the best more than we fear the worst!

We can stand in the presence of somebody far below us morally and not be afraid, but when we stand in the presence of somebody morally upright, we are uncomfortable. *We fear our highest potential!* Why do we evade our own possibilities? Because there is a universal fear of an encounter with God. Maslow called it "counter-valuing"—the fear of a direct confrontation with God. We fear running into God, just as we fear running into our own opportunities and possibilities. So we back away from all of it.

So what's the difference between man and animals?

First, humans have a sense of humor.

Second, humans have the ability to learn and create.

Third, all humans have within themselves undiscovered potential to be more than they are.

Fourth, as the Jewish psychiatrist put it:

"MAN IS THE ONLY ANIMAL THAT HAS
THE ABILITY TO CONCEPTUALIZE GOD."

The process toward success starts when you potential-ize, which means opening yourself to the possibility of God placing in your consciousness a dream, or desire, an idea, an awareness, an opportunity, a challenge. Every achiever I have met says, "My life turned around when I began to believe in me."

Believe in yourself!

There may be significant differences between animals and humans, but all human beings have virtually the same potential. The primary difference among the loser, the moderate achiever, the high achiever, and the perceived genius is what they DO with their potential.

I am honored to be a member of the Horatio Alger and the American Academy of Achievement organizations. I have met and interviewed many if not most of the so-called high-est achievers in the world, and I am sure of this: Most of them have no more potential than you or me.

They have maximized their potential—and so can you!

There are no great people! They all have virtually the same potential. However, they have different ideas, they dream different dreams, they make different commitments. Deep down in their heart, they make different promises. Really.

There are no extra-ordinary people. They're all very ordinary but they make extra-ordinary decisions.

You can be one of them!

The more honestly I study the human being at his or her best, the more convinced I am of the reality of God. The supreme example of humanity at its best, of course, was Jesus when he walked the earth two thousand years ago; although fully divine, he was also fully human and subject to temptation and fraility. In our own time, Billy Graham or Mother Teresa might serve as examples of fine human beings. And only God could generate the kind of spirit that motivates and monitors and manages these spiritually heroic, spectacular human beings.

Somehow these "Power Thought Processors" are connected spiritually with the Master Programmer who "started something out of nothing." Connected to this eternal creative source, the super successful people are networking spiritually with a creative, cosmic command center.

God is Real!

God is Alive!

God is the Ultimate Command Center!

Today I sense this stronger than ever before in my earthly life. I sense it. I feel it. I believe it. On a tiny, small scale, I experience a paradigm that makes this real.

I am one small person who speaks every week in a pulpit called the Crystal Cathedral. My message is taped and aired over 170 television stations in the United States, then sent to be aired on Channel 1 in Moscow. This channel was set up decades ago at the height of the Cold War. Under the dictatorship of the Communist power, under the eye of the KGB, Channel 1 was wired to feed into every single television set in all of the fifteen republics of the U.S.S.R., plus into every television set of all the eastern countries in the

Communist empire—Poland, Hungary, Albania, Czechoslo-vakia, Yugoslavia, Bulgaria, Romania.

The Communist power center wanted to have live communication with every Russian citizen living anywhere in the world. So they created what was and is a collection of satellites in space, connected together, so that a TV program could be beamed up from Channel 1 to Sputnik, thereby connecting to the satellite network that would instantly footprint the entire globe.

I am told that every Sunday my message transmitted over Channel 1 can be seen and heard in every country on this globe—184 nations in all! That boggles my mind—what a communication network!

God operates in an alive, alert, active, aggressive, cosmic system of communication. God is constantly sending POWER THOUGHTS to communicate with all of His human creations who chose by faith (Power Thinking) to connect with Him!

Get connected with God's Cosmic Command Center and feel the <u>Power Thoughts</u> send energy into your turned on personality.

Now you are ready to to <u>maximize your achievement Possibilities</u>.

Your computer is turned on.

<u>On the screen of your imagination the instructions appear, outlining this process called success.</u> Watch the messages come across the screen!

1. POTENTIALIZE, then
2. PRIORITIZE, now

3. POSSIBILITIZE,

4. INTERNALIZE,

5. ORGANIZE,

6. REVITALIZE, and

7. PATRONIZE!

Now press 1.—POTENTIALIZE.

Most people make a fundamental mistake. They set their priorities before they discover what their potential is.

If the first thing I do when I wake up in the morning is set my priorities, then I have made a fundamental mistake. First, I need to consider what I could do, what I could do with the day that is waiting for me. The first thing Power Thinkers do is Potentialize—they look for what they *could* do, what they *could* be.

Do it now! Do it again tomorrow. Do it every day that you are alive. POTENTIALIZE!

I have two of the world's most capable management consultants in my church membership: Jim Kinnu, who was one of the top executives at Northrup Aviation, and John Bradley, the chief management authority at McDonnell-Douglas. Both men have worked with tens of thousands of persons in their corporate management structures. Today these two super professional men are volunteers to critique and restructure the Crystal Cathedral Ministries. Their first assignment to me and my staff of twelve top executives was "Write your Mission Statement."

"This is not easy, " they told me. They were right! It

takes time. It takes real reflective thinking. And it's tempting to skip over this step. But those who neglect to carefully write out their mission statement ultimately will fail to become everything they can be. So I ask you: Have you written out your Mission Statement?

It takes time. Don't rush over this step. Don't skip it. Put this book down and do it before you read on.

WRITE IT DOWN. <u>NOW</u>.

Now, with your Mission Statement written out, before you set goals, begin to potentialize by opening your mind to real creativity.

Ask yourself these questions:

- What would I try to do if I knew I might succeed?

- What goals would I set if I knew I could not fail?

- What price am I willing to pay?

- What sacrifices am I willing to make?
—Would I be willing to move?
—Where would I go?
—What if I changed vocations?

- What *could* I do?
- Where *could* I go?
- What *could* I become?

Write the answers DOWN. Do it *NOW!* You'll feel better about yourself.

Next, check your ABC's of Achievement:

A—<u>APPRAISAL.</u>

Get an up-to-date, new appraisal of this person called YOU.

You are smarter today than you have ever been before. You can learn a lot in a hurry!—if you want to! You can learn to speak in several foreign languages in only a couple of years. <u>Yes</u>, <u>you</u> <u>can</u>!

Answer these questions. Who are you? What are your strengths? What's your experience? Training? Know-how? Where are you weak? How can you upgrade or retrain yourself?

Get out a piece of paper and a pencil and write out an honest appraisal of yourself. Don't be afraid to write something good.

B—<u>BASE.</u>

Your base of strength. Review it! Check your academic, professional, financial and spiritual asset base. What do you have in assets? Could you shift? Would you sell or barter some assets to improve your position?

Would you spend some money on getting more education? My friend Cory SerVass was fifty years old when she earned her M.D. degree. Then she wanted to share her knowledge to help people. So she bought the bankrupt magazine *The Saturday Evening Post* to create a platform so she could teach people better health practices. Every month her article appears in her magazine under her name, Cory SerVass, M.D.

Start listing all the people you know. You will discover a major part of your Power Base in the people you are currently connected with.

C—CONNECTIONS.

Who do you know know that you didn't know yesterday? Last week? Last month? Last year? Connect with what's going on in your world today—listen to the news. Don't read last week's or last month's printout. Your potential changes everyday!!! Listen to the news. Read today's paper! Check the latest magazines. Use the FAX and telephone. Get with it! Grow! Then know that you did grow!

Who would you like to meet and get connected with in a personal, professional, social or spiritual relationship? And how could this positively increase your potential to improve or expand your mission?

Check your up-to-the-minute connections. Your customers, clients, and other connections add up to terrific, silent asset value! Don't under-estimate them. Use them. And thank them. Good people want to be used by good people with good ideas!

What have you done as you potentialized?

You have caught a fresh vision of your mission.

You have asked the right questions.

You have checked your ABC's. And now—

You can see and hear new opportunities, new dreams knocking.

But what if you don't have the time, money or energy to seize these new, exciting options? You say your plans and budgets are already set?

Whatever you do—don't drop the new vision! You must—yes, *you must* take the second step and follow Potentialize with Prioritize. Be ready to reorganize your priorities.

Now press 2.—<u>PRIORITIZE.</u>

Do it! Do it now! Do it every day! Your Potential changes every day.

This is the time to classify your priorities. To really enhance, elaborate or execute your mission, arrange your priorities into one of three categories, columns or files.

When the blueprints of the Crystal Cathedral were submitted and after we had committed ourselves to building it, the cost of construction dramatically shot up, mostly due to inflation and the shocking rise of interest rates. It was then that our chief financial officer, Charles Cringle, came to me and said, "Bob, we're faced with the impossible dream of building this all-glass Cathedral. The cost is really inflating. We don't have the money to finish it in all of its details. I suggest you postpone the finishing touches that could be added at a later date."

"First, prioritize what you <u>must</u> build," he went on. "Second, list what you should <u>build</u>, and finally, write down what you <u>want</u> to build. Prioritize the functions, then the finances, then the construction. It's the only way to complete such a big project."

His wise counsel and expert financial talent saved the dream. Through prioritizing the "musts," the "shoulds" and the "wants," the building of the Cathedral was completed without bankrupting us. Today, we continue to prioritize with these three categories:

1. <u>I Must Do!</u>

This is Priority Number One.

I must do this. No one else <u>can</u> or should or will.

I <u>MUST</u> do this. If I neglect to do this, the mission will be terminated, diminished, or permanently handicapped or aborted.

I must <u>DO</u> this. Before I die! I cannot waste time. I must not abort this God-given dream.

I <u>MUST DO</u> THIS!

2. I really <u>SHOULD</u> do this.

Like: exercise thirty minutes at least three days a week.

Like: Shop for . . .

Like: Telephone ___, write ___, read ___, FAX ___.

Like: Schedule time on my calendar for rest, worship, reading, entertainment, CONTINUING EDUCATION.

3. I <u>WANT TO</u>

get _____,

go _____,

learn _____,

see _____,

do _____,

finish_____,

start _____,

meet _____,

call _____,

write _____,

invest _____.

Now—keep the basics in mind as you Prioritize. Don't

let locked-in thinking blind you in this step. "Locked-in Thinking" could kill you here.

Keep your thinking open to "hear" what you were not expecting to hear at this stage in your life. Evaluate swiftly and very intelligently. Decide firmly, and move ahead forthrightly.

Don't be too proud to:

carry a parachute, or

plan an emergency exit, or

wear a bulletproof vest, or

draft an escape clause, or

organize alternate financing.

But: don't carelessly ignore and reject a fantastic opportunity because your plans, goals, schedules, calendars didn't allow you to grasp this unexpected Potential.

Think!

Prioritize!

All this said, let nothing tempt you to compromise your integrity. Don't lose sight of what's really important.

Once there was a wonderful old professor, but he was a bit on the arrogant side. He met a young boy who was not doing all that well in school. In an attempt to motivate him, the professor took the boy on a weekend canoe trip.

They started out on a strange river, in the dark of the night, because the professor wanted the boy to see all the stars in the skies. "Son," the professor said, "look up. See all the stars? What can you tell me about the stars?"

The boy looked up at the twinkling heavens and said, "Nothing, sir. I know nothing about the stars."

"If you don't know about the stars," the professor said, "you've missed out on one third of life."

When daylight came, and they drifted down river, the branch of a tree reached out above their little canoe. The professor pulled a leaf off the tree. He showed the veins of the leaf to the boy. He pointed out the shape, the color and the texture. Then he said, "What do you know about trees and plants and flowers?"

The boy once again answered, "Nothing, sir."

"Then you've missed out on another third of life," the professor said.

Then the water became shallow and the professor reached down and his hand came up with his fingers separated and on his open palm there glistened a shimmering, wet stone. And he said, "What do you know about rocks, my boy?"

The boy said, "Nothing, sir."

The professor shook his head in disappointment. "You know nothing about the stars, nothing about plants, nothing about earth and stones. You missed out on another third of life."

Just then, they heard a noise downstream.

The boy looked at the professor and said, "Sir, what do you know about swimming?"

"Nothing," the professor answered.

With that, the boy dove into the water and started swimming toward the shore.

"Wait!" called the professor. "Where are you going?"

The boy's head flicked around as he said, "That's a waterfall downstream, and you just missed out on all of life!"

Remember this. In setting Priorities, learn the lessons of ethics and morality or you can lose everything!

That's a basic truth!

If you haven't learned that essential lesson, you cannot swim the risky river called life.

What's really important? What really matters? As you prioritize make sure your values are solid and sterling.

Make sure your life is uncompromising as far as your treasured relationships are concerned.

PRIORITIZE

But—

DON'T GIVE UP YOUR PRIVATE PRAYER TIME.

You'll need the guidance, wisdom, courage that
only God can provide.

PRIORITIZE

But—

DON'T SACRIFICE YOUR MARRIAGE AND YOUR CHILDREN
IN THE PROCESS.

The busiest men I know still control their
calendars and schedule their children's
birthdays and major school events.

PRIORITIZE

MAKE SURE YOUR PERSPECTIVE REALLY PUTS
FIRST THINGS FIRST.

Now, you see Potential you never saw before. You've PRIORITIZED—you've readjusted your time—your money—your energy—your calendar.

Now press 3.—POSSIBILITIZE.

You have POTENTIALIZED. You have caught an
    expanded vision.
You have PRIORITIZED. Suddenly, the new potential
    takes top place in your priorities. You have re-
    prioritized your time, your money and your
    relationships with people.

Now—you will have to POSSIBILITIZE: You bluntly,
    boldly, beautifully face the problems you have
    just created for yourself.

Congratulations. You have created problems for your-
self!
For you allowed the light to go on in your head.
You dared to think bigger than you ever have before.
You made your thinking big enough for God to fit in.
You are turned on by a new dream.
You have suddenly seen something so important that
you've rearranged and reestablished priorities.
How can you do this?
Can you change your priorities?
Postpone the lunch you had on the calendar?
Give the tickets away?
Don't be intimidated. Dare to make changes!
"People who never change their minds are either
perfect—or stubborn." You don't belong to either of these
groups.

Can you reestablish priorities and not lose integrity?! Reputation?! Respect?

Can you really Seize the Potential; rearrange, reprioritize, reschedule time, money, relationships, promises, rewrite contracts, agreements, plans, commitments—?

Impossible?!?

Wait a minute! Everything you are—and all you will amount to rides on this moment.

You must become a sudden expert as a problem solving person.

You are ready to Possibilitize.

What's that?

Possibilitizing is managing by magnificent assumptions. That's Possibility Thinking. That's assuming leadership over your dreams and your destiny.

You face impossible problems?

Problems are illusions—in reality they are only decisions waiting to be made by the top person and that's you.

Possibilitize. How's that? (1) Choose to keep the potential alive. Don't surrender leadership to foes, fears, fences or frightening fantasies. (2) Reject, expel, cut out this devastating word "impossible." Replace that one knee-jerk, negative, reactionary word with these wiser, smarter, braver, potent words:

"It might be possible if—"
"It might be possible with—"
"It might be possible when—"
"It might be possible after—"
"It might be possible, however—"

Think! Imagine! Assume! Believe! Execute leadership.

Leadership is the force that sets the goals;
casts the deciding vote;
saves the vision from the fog;
keeps the dream from dropping into a black hole.
There are black holes surrounding all of us!

Possibilitize! Practice Possibility Thinking! Turn every problem into a decision!

Write your "problems" down. Put them in a box labeled: "Decisions I have to make."

"Decisions I'm honored by God to execute and carry out."

"God has chosen me to be entrusted to carry out His dream."

I am a leader. I dared to create these challenges.

I saw a vision—I Potentialized.

I sized up the vision—I Prioritized.

I've seized the vision—I'll Possibilitize.

Now I'll be a match for the mountains I've picked out for myself.

I'll buy, beg, barter or borrow; I'll rent or invent the resources—intellectual, emotional, financial, technical—that I need to succeed.

I'll pray, pay and play—to do what I must do!

I'll really be smart. Watch me. I'll channel and control these challenges that I courageously created by potentializing and then prioritizing.

Now the fun starts. The game is called "Possibilitizing."

Remember the one rule of the game.

NOTHING IS IMPOSSIBLE!

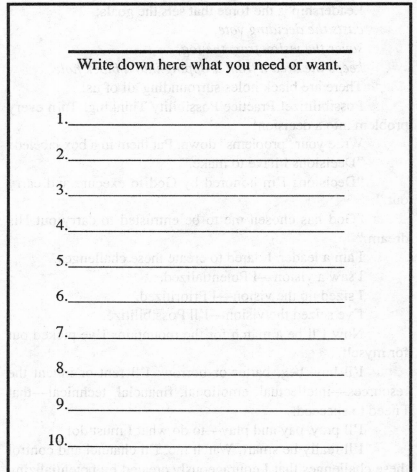

Write down here what you need or want.

1._____

2._____

3._____

4._____

5._____

6._____

7._____

8._____

9._____

10._____

Fill in the ten blanks above with ways to achieve what you need or really want to achieve. Think BIG! Think long—months—years! Think "way out." Pray! Give God a chance to lead you.

Play the Possibility Game and Win! Take a piece of paper. On the top write down what you don't have, but must have, and can't imagine how, where or when, or through whom you can acquire it. Now write down on the left side of the sheet the numbers 1, 2, 3, 4, 5, 6, 7, 8, 9, 10. Now pray: "God, show me ten ways to turn my impossibility into a Possibility. Amen."

I did this when I started my church with two members— my wife and myself—and $500.00. That's all the money I had. I owned no house. My cheap car was mortgaged. I was "hired" by my denomination (the denomination of Norman Vincent Peale). They bought a house for $8,000 and let me live there. They promised me an annual salary of $2,400, or $200 a month. I accepted.

I had a dream! I learned then that <u>nobody has a money problem—it's always an idea problem</u>. Get the right idea and money will be attracted to you!

So I <u>started</u> from <u>scratch</u>. I scrawled on the top of this piece of paper what I needed: A Place to Meet and Start a Church. I flung open the mental doors and windows of my imagination. I wrote down 1 to 10. I prayed. I waited.

Ideas came.

Good ones—and not-so-good ones.

Wild ones.

Different ones.

I wrote them down. One by one I tried each idea—and failed. Until I got to "No. 9—Use a Drive-In Theater." Wild. I tried. The owner said "Yes." The rent? Only ten dollars a week to pay the sound man. That "open-air church" would be my church on Sunday mornings for over five years! I'd

fall in love with the sun, and sky, and trees, and birds, and flowers. Yes, twenty-five years later. We started in 1955 and in 1980 we moved into the Crystal Cathedral. All glass! Ceilings and walls! I wanted to be able to see the sun and sky again. And watch the clouds sliding silently through the soundless sea of space.

How and where did we ever get the support? The help? The money to build a cathedral? Again, I played the game! The architect said I would need $7 million. I wrote it on a piece of paper. I wrote down 1 to 10. I prayed. I threw the windows and doors of my mind open to God. I listened to every idea that came in my mind. I had learned that ideas are everything! I had no money problems—only ideas were needed. I believed God would send them to me through prayer, or through people, or through problems that would force me to think bigger thoughts than I'd ever imagined before!

I started from scratch and scratched it out!

I wrote on a piece of paper:

Ten Ways to Get $7,000,000:

1. Get one gift of $7 million from one person. Laugh! I did! But that relaxed me! I was playing a game and enjoying it! So I relaxed! That set the stage for my subconscious to be creative/receptive to great God-sent ideas.

2. Get seven gifts of one million each from seven people.

3. Get 1 gift of $1 million from one person.
    Get 2 gifts of $500,000 from two persons.
    Get 4 gifts of $250,000 from four persons.

Get 10 gifts of $100,000 from ten persons.
(This would add up to $4 million from seventeen people.)
  4. Sell memorial windows!
  I called the architect. "How many windows are in the Crystal Cathedral?" "10,760!" If we would sell each window for $500 x 10,000 = $5,000,000!! That's exactly what we did—and raised $5 million.
  Not only that, we did get a "Lead-off Gift" of one million dollars cash!
  Then I thought, "We'll have a million-dollar offering Sunday." (This idea was really exciting!) Some years before, I had inherited $10,000 from my father. I invested it in real estate I bought for $30,000. Now before the "million-dollar" Sunday, I sold it for $170,000. I paid off the remaining mortgage of $20,000 and gave a cashier's check for the balance of $150,000 to the church board and challenged them to match it. So my deceased father made the first gift that made possible a successful million-dollar offering on a single Sunday morning!
  Possibilitizing works! I know it . . . I've tried it . . . and a beautiful, sparkling Crystal Cathedral stands today because of a simple, life-changing, power-producing game. It's fun! It's challenging! Play it! No one loses in this game!

  Now press 4.—INTERNALIZE.

  It's time to get enthusiastic. The process of Power Thinking must move from the head to the heart.
  You had a dream—now the dream has you.
  There's a profound, powerful Bible verse you can understand here. "It is <u>God</u> at work <u>in you</u>." (Phil. 2:13)

That's enthusiasm! The word is derived from two Greek words, *en* and *theos*. "In God–ism" is the literal translation. God–in You! I was fascinated to hear my first sermon translated into Russian. It was amazing to hear the English word "enthusiasm" translated into the Russian word—guess what? Enthusiasm! It is the same word in Russian and in English.

Read the rest of the Bible verse. "It is God at work in you, <u>giving you the will</u>." Absolutely—enthusiasm is the core of the WILL-TO-BE and TO DO. Continue reading this verse. "It is God at work in you, <u>giving you</u> the will and <u>the POWER</u>." Enthusiasm is probably the greatest emotional power to motivate creative minds.

Enthusiasm is power.

"Stay-with-it" power

"Start-over-again" power

"Scale back and hold on" power

"Don't get angry or depressed" power

"Break-through thinking" power

Now finish reading this psychologically and theologically powerful sentence from the Bible. "It is God at work in you, giving you the will and the power <u>to achieve His purpose</u>." Fantastic! We are connected to the Master Programmer! If we choose to allow Him, He will enable us to achieve his positive purpose!

Enthusiasm works—even in professions and walks of life that are seemingly nonemotional. Take, for instance, bankers. Wouldn't you say they're objective? Not easily influenced by matters of the heart? Enthusiasm isn't a necessary attribute to be a successful financier.

Well, listen to this story of a famous banker and then tell me what you think.

I sat at a long dinner with the chairman and CEO of Bank of America, Richard M. Rosenberg. I said, "Mr. Rosenberg, I knew and was a good friend of the founder of your bank. He was one of my television fans who became a great friend."

Mr. Rosenberg looked at me, surprised, and said, "You knew Mr. Giannini?"

"No," I said, "I didn't know Mr. Giannini, but the founder of Bank of America wasn't Giannini, it was Walter Braunschweiger."

He shook his head, positively convinced that I was wrong. So, I proceeded to tell him the story.

"First, let me tell you, sir," I said, "I know the history of Bank of America very well. And enthusiasm built your bank." I had his attention.

Walter Braunschweiger started out as the son of a clothing salesman. He went to night school to earn his M.B.A. and law degree. He earned a reputation as a super salesman and went on to found the Bank of America.

Mr. Rosenberg listened carefully as I told him the story I had heard from Walter himself.

A. P. Giannini had founded a very successful bank in the state of California and called it Bank of Italy. Walter and several of his associates thought a bank with the name Bank of America would be more appealing to the midwesterners who had moved to California. They applied for a charter and Walter returned home from San Francisco with the charter in his hands. It read "Bank of America." Walter knew it would be a success. It

71

was! So much so that Mr. Giannini wanted the name himself. They negotiated, they merged, and Walter found himself in a top executive slot.

One Sunday noon during World War II he got a call from Mr. Giannini. "Walter, we know that when the war is over this state will boom. We've got to get ready for the expansion—now! We must borrow fifty million dollars immediately!"

His decision-making voice was filled with urgency. He went on, "Walter, there's only one place to raise that kind of money—the big New York investment boys." Mr. Giannini paused a moment before he dropped his blockbuster: "Tomorrow at one o'clock they're meeting in New York. You will go there, Walter, address them, and sell them on buying this investment opportunity.'"

Braunschweiger was speechless. He knew that such a presentation usually required weeks, perhaps months of research and documentation, to say nothing of the need to carefully mind-condition the men who would be making the decision.

"I knew I couldn't think or say the word impossible to the boss. But I did say, 'Pardon me, sir, but how will I get to New York by one o'clock?'" He knew that, with wartime requirements, airline reservations were needed weeks ahead of time. Furthermore, in that pre-jet age, a flight would take nearly twelve hours.

"It's all arranged, Walter. I've called the airline president. They'll have a seat for you on the night flight leaving San Diego. You'll be in New York early in the morning. You can spend this afternoon gathering the vital facts for a formal presentation. You can outline it on the plane. Rehearse the details carefully! Remember that every fact must be spelled out in precise and accurate detail or you'll violate federal law by making erroneous claims for the sale of stocks." Walter scrambled to collect the data—assets, net worth, liabilities, growth statistics, etc. He also made the plane.

In the early darkness of Monday morning the plane suddenly descended and made an unscheduled stop in St. Louis, Missouri. What happened next was a nightmare! Walter was bumped off to make room for an army general! He watched the dreams of the company disappear as the plane took off and left him—alone in an empty airport.

Desperately he called the boss. "Don't worry, Walter, I'll arrange something." He did. He chartered a special plane. Four hours later Walter was airborne. But could he make the one o'clock meeting? It was nearly twelve noon when he put down at La Guardia, caught a cab, and feverishly rehearsed the intricacies of his finely detailed and legally accurate presentation. As the cab stopped at the Manhattan address, he was horrified to realize he was still dressed in the suit and shirt he had pulled on the day before and slept in all night. Bristles were sprouting on his face. But he had no time. He dashed in, caught an elevator, and with only moments to spare reached the corridor outside the meeting room. He reached for his written presentation. It was gone! In the hectic rush he had left it in the cab.

"Mr. Braunschweiger?" He was being called. What could he do? "One financial misstatement and we could go to prison," he thought. He prayed silently and the inspiration came. "Just be enthusiastic." But could conservative, unemotional, calculating investment bankers respond to enthusiasm?

"How many of you gentlemen have ever been to California?" he began.

The dark-suited, unsmiling, frozen faces drew unanimous blanks.

"Gentlemen," he continued, "it's a gorgeous state built on sunshine and balmy ocean breezes! Miles of orange groves with their waxen leaves shower the air with fragrant perfume in the winter months. Gentle sunshine falls warm on the skin, turning white faces into warm, brown, suntanned smiles. From Iowa, Illinois, Indiana, Minnesota, the tourists come, every frozen January, to bask in this green-flowering garden state, and they spend their money. Finally, when spring thaws the ice in Chicago, they go back, leaving behind millions of dollars, money that never again moves east but stays there in the sunshine to form a growing, swelling, bulging pool of money as momentous as a vast, undeveloped, underground ocean of oil!"

By this time Walter's enthusiasm was really carrying him along! He did not make a single precise statement but concluded: "Now gentlemen, when the war is over, and it will be soon, the boys who have been stationed in California will come back to live here. The state will mushroom and Bank of America, chartered to establish branches, will build branches in all of these booming new communities! We will be ready to take in all that money! And I'm giving you the first opportunity to make an investment in what is sure to be one of the world's great banks."

His report was finished. What happened next is history. That group of cautious financiers bought the entire stock issue—to the last dollar! Enthusiasm made a fifty-million-dollar sale! Bank of America's future exploded—then and there!

Walter Braunschweiger unlocked enthusiasm and with this persuasive power helped turn the Bank of America from a modestly successful bank into one of the most powerful financial enterprises in the world. Possibility thinking generates enthusiasm and no man has ever calculated the dynamism of this spiritual force.

Enthusiasm—Don't knock it!
—Don't block it!
—Unlock it!

Superachievers reach a point where they allow themselves to be consumed by this marvelous, motivating energy!

They have internalized their project! They would probably die for it!

Disappointed? Yes! Discouraged? Never!

Disappointment is a common, normal human experience. Everyone has tasted this. If you have never been disappointed you were probably aiming too low or moving too slow.

Robert Browning said, "A man's reach should exceed his grasp, or what's a heaven for?"

Discouragement is a chosen, negative reaction to disappointment and the taproot of enthusiasm can't let this happen. The spirit of enthusiasm comes back at low times.

The spark breaks out in a fresh flame.

The instrument is in tune again.

The blade is sharpened.

Enthusiasm won't let you quit. God is at work in you, giving you the <u>will</u> and the <u>power</u> to achieve His purpose.

75

Now press 5.—<u>ORGANIZE.</u>

IF YOU CAN DREAM IT—YOU CAN DO IT!

You can do it even though everyone—including you—thinks "It's impossible." Every single dream I've ever had was impossible when I first dreamed it.

I learned this lesson:

"NOTHING IS IMPOSSIBLE"

      —If I get smarter people to help me.
      —If I'm willing to share the credit.
      —If I get my ego out of the way.
      —If I get organized to succeed!

I've learned how to succeed—but not without strong help from good people.

The story of my life is the right people with the right support who came along at the right time unsolicited, but not unrecognized, by me.

In the first thirty-eight years of my ministry, that sentence says it all. It's awesome how the specialized, skilled support came just when I needed it. I am awestruck at the unseen hand of God in my life again and again and again and again. It never stops or fails.

I've often said to my wife, who is the <u>only living adult</u> who has been with me through every phase of my life and work, "Honey, if I ever write an autobiography, I'll have to give it the title *The Right Person at the Right Spot at the Right Time.*"

My ministry would never have happened without dozens of strategic persons who alone kept the Process of Success progressing. Architects, designers, real estate agents, financial experts, psychiatrists and psychologists. Publishers. Television producers. Theologians. Global power players. Norman Vincent Peale. Billy Graham. Fulton Sheen. Richard Neutra. Philip Johnson. Victor Frankl. John Crean. W. Clement Stone. Rupert Murdoch. Armand Hammer. The list goes on and on. How could it happen so successfully?

I got organized. So can you. How?

1. HUMILITY IS THE FIRST STEP.

Absolutely nothing is more important than confronting the damnable, demolishing power of egotistical denial, "I can do it—alone." Admit that "it's impossible" without help from a Higher Power. Every member of Alcoholics Anonymous knows this. The Beatitudes of Jesus are unmatched sentences of life-changing wisdom. They became the backbone of the Twelve Steps used by Alcoholics Anonymous.

The first Beatitude is *"Blessed are the poor in spirit, for theirs is the kingdom of heaven."* (Matthew 5:3) In my book on the Beatitudes, I call this the opening sentence for successful living. For it teaches this primary principle that underlies all achievement. Understand it. Organize your life around it. Here it is. Talk to yourself and repeat it out loud.

"I NEED HELP! I CAN'T DO IT ALONE."

"Nothing is impossible"—if I'm humble enough, and smart enough to get the right people to help me.

I count as one of my greatest honors my election into the Horatio Alger organization. I think everyone who gets elected thinks they don't deserve to be a member, but they accept with gratitude and humility.

The first qualification is that you had to begin with virtually nothing. A lot of the supersuccessful people that you know in this country today are not eligible because they had inherited money or position. All Horatio Alger winners started from nothing,

In 1992 I introduced a new winner of the Horatio Alger award. His name was Tom Harken. I got to know him and spent some time with him. His is an amazing story of success. When he was twelve years of age, he contracted tuberculosis, got polio and was in an iron lung for one year.

I asked him, "When you got sick, is it true that you dropped out of school and you couldn't read or write? You never did learn to read but you didn't tell anybody? How could you keep that a secret?"

"It was very difficult, Bob, and I was ashamed of it for many, many years. There's no question about it. I still am ashamed of it. I could not read or write. But I married a great gal, Melba."

"Did she know you were illiterate when she married you?"

"Yes, she did."

"When did you have the nerve to tell her?"

"She had to fill out the marriage license. I couldn't do it."

"Tell me about those difficult years when you were so sick as a boy."

"I spent months in the hospital and when I finally got out of the hospital, I was quarantined in my family's home in one room. For the next three years I didn't see anybody."

I interrupted him, "Three years?"

"Yes, and after I got out of that quarantine, I still was kept isolated because they were afraid that I'd give it to somebody or my brothers or sisters, so I was just locked in a room all by myself. When I went back to school, I was in the twenty-third week of the seventh grade and I was too far behind. I told my dad, 'Dad, I can't take it anymore. I just can't take it. I'm going to quit.'"

"And he said, 'Well, you're going to make it, son. You're going to climb that ladder of success and you're going to make it, because you're a good talker and you're a worker.' I replied, 'Yes, sir, I'm not scared of work.'

"Then Dad gave me two bits of advice. One of them was, 'always believe in God, and believe in Jesus Christ.' I've done that. The other was 'marry a smart woman.' I mean to tell you, Dr. Schuller, I did that. Melba was valedictorian of her class. And she's a great lady."

"So—you married a smart woman, but you had no diploma and you couldn't read or write. What kind of job could a kid like you get?"

"Well, I couldn't fill out any applications—and the only job I didn't have to fill out any application for was a vacuum salesman, so I sold vacuum cleaners, and I was good at it!"

"You sold door-to-door, didn't you?"

"You bet! I knocked on a hundred doors a day in order to show one vacuum cleaner, and maybe, maybe I'd sell one."

79

"But if you sold one, you'd have to write down the name and what it cost and all of that, didn't you? "

"Now there was the problem. I was good with numbers, but I couldn't fill out the application. So I had to remember everything they told me, such as bank accounts, where they bought their car, where they bought their homes. If they did business with Sears or whoever. Then when I'd come home late at night, my wife, Miss Melba, would meet me at the back door, and the kids would already be asleep. I'd go give them a hug and kiss and then she'd say, 'Well, honey, did you sell one?' I'd say, 'You bet, I sure did.' And she would sit down with me to fill out all the details of the contract. This is the way we did it for many, many years.

"I became a director of a bank. I became a director of a hospital. I became part owner of a bank. Nobody knew all those years that I was illiterate until the Horatio Alger night. On May 1st of 1992, they found out. That's when I finally told the world that I'd been illiterate all of those years.

"Dr. Schuller, illiteracy is a terrible, terrible thing. It really, really hurts to be illiterate. You can't open up a menu at a restaurant, you can't read what you want to eat. You can't go through a city and know what city you're going through. My wife and I kept this a secret until December 10, 1991. We took our two boys, who are now grown men, into our boardroom and told them the truth.

"The hardest part of my illiteracy was when my two boys would climb up on my lap on a Sunday night—this was the only day I wasn't working—and they wanted me to read them a bedtime story. Melba would grab those boys and say, 'Let me read it to you.' The only thing I could read was, 'See

Spot run.' And let me tell you, I felt like running right off the face of the earth. It was a sad, sad day for me. And it was a sad day for Melba.

"But I got over that, Dr. Schuller, with faith in the Good Lord. And today—let me tell you—today I can take any book and I can read every page of it, thanks to Miss Melba. And when my grandchildren climb in my lap, and ask me to read them a book, I don't have to pretend or ask someone else to do it for me. I tell you—it chokes me up, just thinking about it.

"You just can't imagine it. I never finished grade school—or high school! I never had a senior prom. I never had parties. Imagine my joy when the the superintendent of the high school in a little town called Lakeview, Michigan, where I was born and raised, called up my office and said, 'Mr. Harken, would you come and graduate with the class of 1992?' I said, 'You've got to be kidding. You mean dress up with the hat and gown and process down the aisle?' He said to me, 'Not only that, you're going to be the speaker.' I said, 'I'll do it. I'll do it. I'll do it.' And I did it. I'm now a high school graduate. Isn't that something? Dr. Schuller, anything is possible!"

Tom and I locked eyes. "Tom," I said, "people who are grateful are driven by helping others who are where they are, right? And, what really turns you on now is to help fight the problem of illiteracy in others, right?"

"You bet!" Tom Harken said.

"I heard about how you helped a kid who was kicked out of college."

"Yes. A young man called me up and said, 'I need

your help, Mr. Harken. I've started my second year at Baylor University, and believe it or not, I'm illiterate.'"

"How could he get that far, Tom?"

"Friends helped him. Even his mother and father never knew it. But that young man is going in the right direction today. We're helping lots of people who are illiterate."

And you, too, can help! Everyone can reach out and help somebody who is having trouble with reading and writing. Just help them.

2. ORGANIZE WITH THE "HELP-HELP" ATTITUDE.

Some call it "Win-Win." That's great! I prefer "Help-Help."

The secret of success is still simple.

Find a need and fill it.

Find a hurt and heal it.

Find a problem and solve it.

Find a worker—and help him or her, too.

That's what Tom Harken did! He found a wife who needed a good husband who could be a good provider and a good father for the children she helped to mother. She found a man who needed a smart, educated partner to make it in the world—as a success and in the family as a strong mother to the children he helped to father.

"Help-Help" is the basic principle for organizing the people without whom your progress would be aborted, dwarfed or sidetracked!

The most successful entrepreneur in Orange County, California, in 1955, when I arrived here, was Walter Knott, founder of a world-class tourist attraction called Knotts Berry

Farm—a multi-million-dollar supersuccessful enterprise. Walter and I became and remained close friends until his death.

The secret of his success? Why, it was his mission statement "to create great job opportunities for people who love to entertain, amuse and feed tourists who want a good time when they come to California."

Help—create jobs for people!

Help—to create a good time for tourists!

Help-Help! And it worked wonders! Guess what? The result for Walter Knott was called "Healthy Profit."

Walter was "turned on" and "tuned in" to helping people help themselves by helping others. He organized his life around this passion for people. So his primary goal was to create job opportunities. "It costs me $5,000 in capital outlay to create one full-time job opportunity," he boasted proudly yet humbly to me. (That was thirty years ago.) "That's why I am not living in a big mansion, and I don't buy superexpensive cars. When I think what these dollars will do to create one or two more job opportunities—you know where I'll put my cash." And he really lived by that "Help-Help" principle.

3. ORGANIZE AROUND BASIC, CLASSICAL, FUNDAMENTAL NEEDS.

Understand what the real need really is.

Railroads failed when they thought they were in the railroad business. The truth is they were in the transportation business and when they forgot that fact they lost to competition that could transport not just on rails but on planes and trucks and boats.

Pastors failed when they thought they were in a "denominational" or "theological" business. The truth is they're in the business to inspire and motivate human beings with "Faith, Hope, and Love, and the greatest of these is love." (I Corinthians 13:13)

My good friend Bruce Larson, the co-pastor at the Crystal Cathedral, told me the story about a successful factory that made drills. One day the owner of the factory called his top four vice presidents together and announced he was going to retire. At that point, the vice presidents all sat up expectantly, waiting to hear who had been chosen to replace the owner.

"I've chosen my son as my successor," the owner said.

At the next meeting, the son was present and presiding. He addressed the four vice presidents and asked them, "What are your goals for the company for the next five to ten years?"

One vice president offered, "Well, sir, we're looking at new shapes and sizes for our drills. The competition is stiff, and we've got to come up with new and better products to stay competitive."

Then the new president dropped a bombshell. "Now that I've taken over, I have news for you: We are no longer going to sell drills."

The vice presidents were astounded. No more drills? What could he possibly be thinking? Two of the vice presidents started thinking about updating their résumés.

"What are we going to sell?" one vice president bravely asked.

"We are going to sell holes," the new president

announced. "People don't want to buy drills. They want to buy what drills do for them. They want to buy holes."

The company succeeded under the new president because they began to think of other high-tech ways of creating holes. That company developed lasers long before anyone else was even thinking about the technology of drilling and cutting with light. Everyone else was still thinking about "drills." The company expanded and succeeded.

4. BELIEVE.

Organize your life and work around positive principles and positive people.

If you will follow this principle, you will turn a failure into a success, and an impossibility into a possibility.

Herman Cain has a reputation for being one of the great turn-around corporate chiefs in America. "What is your secret?" I asked him. His answer?

"Well, Dr. Schuller, it's really not a secret. First, it's my belief in God and in Jesus Christ. And, if you have that belief, you can then believe in yourself.

"Because <u>believing in yourself means that you are an instrument through which God makes things happen</u>.

"Whenever I've been faced with a turn-around situation, <u>I first organize</u> to find out who the people are in the organization that believe that the company can succeed. Then I give everyone an opportunity to make the right decision.

"Those that decide that the company can succeed, they stay.

"Those who believe that the company cannot succeed, we redirect their career. Because it only takes one negative person in an organization to kill what you are trying to achieve when everybody else believes in it."

I once asked a supersuccessful high school administrator how he accomplished so much in the school, in our community and in his professional organizations. His answer was really smart! "I never do anything if I can hire someone else who knows how to do it better than I can. Then I never tell them what to do. I give them great freedom to excel. So I'm never overwhelmed, but free and uncluttered to do what I and only I can do, must do and really want to do."

Great advice! Follow it and you'll find your failures will become successes! Your impossibilities are becoming possibilities!

What kind of talent, skill, spirit, do you need? Hire them.

Or rent them for special projects. They're available. They're called "consultants."

I am successful because I have learned to hire people who are smarter than I am to perform critical services in crucial times.

The job of organizing is never "wrapped up."

For change is constant and inevitable. So great lives and institutions are never organized—they are always in the process of reorganizing!

Prediction! You'll help a lot of people! And be successful enough to move to the highest level! You'll become a patron! A philanthropist! If you'll just keep revitalized! Renewed! Ever enthusiastic!

Now press 6.—<u>REVITALIZE.</u>

Enthusiasm can run out.

There are limits to every person's emotional energy.

Then you'll need to:

Refuel.

Revitalize.

Success doesn't eliminate all problems. In fact, it frequently creates new ones.

Watch out for "burnout." Protect against it. Keep your exciting new life balanced in your enthusiastic adventure. Take time once a week to worship, rest and meditate.

The human being was designed to run six days. Then it would be out of gas—needing refueling. Don't mess around with this carefully engineered soul that you are.

My wife has always kept Monday nights on my calendar for a "date" with her. Just the two of us, alone. To laugh, to lift our spirits, to love. We were married in 1950 and no marriage is more fulfilling and satisfying than ours, well over forty years later. All of our five children grew up thinking that all families went to church for a good time every Sunday, and that parents always got babysitters so they—Dad and Mom—could go out every Monday night. All five of our children are happily married and following the exciting example they learned as children.

Keep life balanced and you'll never have burnout.

For a short time the power might go out. But don't call it a burnout, or you'll quit. It's only a temporary power shortage. In the public utilities corporations, this is called a "brown-out." Don't make the mistake of calling a "brown-out" a "burnout." Power can and will be restored.

Yes, I've had times when I've experienced power shortages. When my daughter lost a leg. When my wife had a mastectomy. When I had an accident in Amsterdam.

I was found in a coma on my hotel balcony. I was whisked by ambulance to a hospital where they rushed me to surgery. They shaved the hair, cut the scalp, drilled through the skull bone. A broken vein had been bleeding for ten hours and I was told later by the doctor that in twenty minutes I would have been dead.

I came out of surgery not knowing where I was, why I was there, or what had happened. All I could think of was a line. A sentence entered my brain as I awoke from my anesthesia. It was a fabulous line.

I'm a writer. When a new "line" comes into my brain—out of the blue—I take it as a "gift" from my Master Programmer. A "gift" from God. He wants it to be used! He trusts me with it. <u>I must!</u> <u>I must!</u> I must grab it, treasure it, keep it, use it, share it! I called the nurse. I didn't realize that I couldn't speak. I wanted desperately to tell her the line and have her write it down.

But I couldn't talk. I didn't know why, so I closed my eyes and kept repeating the line over and over until I had it. The next day my wife arrived on an emergency flight from Los Angeles. She knew I was trying to say something. All she could hear was a jumble of sounds from my mouth. I couldn't speak.

"Give him a pen and paper," she said. They did. I could not even form a single letter. My wife saved the scribble.

The next day, I still could not speak. I took another piece of paper—and tried once again to write the line.

So it was for the next day and the next day and the next day and the next. After seven days, my wife said to the doctor, "My husband is a professional speaker. When will he be able to speak again?"

"We don't know, Mrs. Schuller," the doctors told her. "We can't make any promises."

"My husband is a professional writer. When will he be able to write again?"

His shoulders shrugged. "We just don't know—when—if—even . . ." was his answer, adding, "I think we have a problem here, Mrs. Schuller. I think we should take him in—soon—for a second surgery. Will you approve?"

I was a professional speaker and I couldn't speak.

I was a professional writer and I couldn't write.

The eighth day, another operation. A second brain surgery.

I continued to focus my brain continually for all of these eight days on the one sentence I'd been given when I awakened from my first operation.

I awoke from my second brain surgery in eight days. Again my wife gave me a pen and paper. And she prayed. Outside my fourth-floor window she saw it—a sparrow fluttering against the glass! It would not leave. In her mind came another thought—a second POWER THOUGHT—from God. *Your husband is saved and will be well.*

She turned. She saw me smile. As she took from me the paper, she could read my writing. Here is that sentence.

"HOW SWEET IT IS TO STAND ON THE EDGE OF TOMORROW"

Power was back on! Revitalized! If you keep the faith, if you keep the dream, then watch!

You'll see:

- There is a new bloom on the rose.
- There is a sharp edge on the blade.
- The piano is back in tune.
- The trumpet sounds clear again.
- The youthful enthusiasm has returned!

HOW DO YOU KEEP REVITALIZED? RENEWED? RE-ENERGIZED?

First of all, expect to have tough times. Don't be surprised, shaken, or discouraged when you run into them.

1. Decide to restore and renew your spirit. Remember: Enthusiasm is a <u>choice!</u>

2. Polish the windows of your spirit. Use what works for you. Music, cassettes, video, audio, prayer.

3. Feed and fuel the heart. Choose entertainment and enjoy fellowship with positive people.

4. Clean up your act. Make sure you haven't allowed a negative-thinking, cynical, suspicious, pollution-infected culture to infiltrate.

5. Polish your positive relationships. Make connections with positive people. They're out there. Meet them. Reconnect. Write notes. Make telephone calls.

6. Tune in to the Power Thoughts in the last part of this book. Read the Bible. Collect a book for your own heart's needs.

7. Set new goals—you'll die without them.

One of the most important assignments of my pastoral life happened when the family of Vice President Hubert Humphrey called me.

"Dr. Schuller," they said, "the doctor tells Hubert that he has only a few months to live. He does not want to go back to Washington. We think he should. Could you fly to Minnesota and visit him and try to talk him into going back for a last time to the capital? He's always responded to you."

As the plane landed I was really uneasy: Why had I agreed to come here? If his family couldn't get him to go, what made me think I could? I really didn't believe that I could. I prayed. "God, you do it. I can't. Amen."

When I entered his apartment, I was shocked. How long had it been? Was it nine years since he first wrote to me and asked for a copy of my Possibility Thinker's Creed? Had nine years passed since I first met this dynamic man? All of these years I had been his pastor by way of television. But now, he was so sick. How could I motivate him to go back to Washington, D.C., one last time?

I was amazed at how God answered my prayer.

"Hubert," I said, "when you were really down—how did you always manage to come back again? When Richard Nixon defeated you for President—by only a few hundred thousand votes, how did you find renewal again?"

"Oh, my notebook, Bob," he answered. "Muriel, where's my little black notebook? You know the one."

Muriel jumped up, moved fast, left the room, and returned with a small leather-bound notebook. It was fat, bulging with little loose notes and clippings inside. He carefully removed the rubber band and started reading. "Here's yours," he said to me, and he read the Possibility Thinker's Creed by Robert Schuller:

When faced with a mountain,

I WILL NOT QUIT!
I will keep on striving
until
I climb over,
find a pass through,
tunnel underneath,
or
simply stay
and
turn the mountain
into a gold mine
with
God's help!!

Suddenly, I thought I saw a returning spark in his eyes. The memory power system had been turned on again. I cried out, "Hubert, you've got to go back once more."

Shocking all of us, he said, "Muriel, I think I will."

Muriel smiled broadly and said, "Hubert, I'll call President Carter. He's in San Francisco. I'm sure he'll pick you up and take you back on Air Force One."

The next day Air Force One landed in Minneapolis.

A thin, weak, but still handsome, smiling Senator Humphrey walked aboard.

The President welcomed him warmly.

Revitalized!

Never, never, never give up heart!

Now press 7.—PATRONIZE.

Patronize is a powerful word to Positive Thinkers. It means we now live—to give!

You've reached the top! Here you will feel the glorious flush of satisfying success!

You will become a patron. A philanthropist.

This is where living is giving. The joy of giving is the crowning purpose of living.

You're really a success when you "start to give something back."

You and I and every living human being owe so much to so many that we can never give too much back.

"I made it—all by myself" was the proud boast of a very wealthy corporate achiever.

"But you owe a lot to many who helped you get here," I suggested, adding, "Once a man loved a woman and they married and you were conceived by them and you were born!"

Some pioneers carved this country out of wilderness and wrote a Bill of Rights to allow you freedom to dream and do.

Some person worked, studied, and wrote the books you read to become educated.

Some teachers taught you to read, to write and add and subtract.

Some doctors saved your life with inoculations against diseases like smallpox or polio.

Some men—young men—were called to keep enemy soldiers from running over this world in the armies of insane dictators. They sacrificed their lives for you to enjoy the freedom that was and is your birthright.

Someone even prayed for you. You have no idea who all prayed for you. Was it your mother? Father? Neighbor? Teacher? You will never know.

How often did God Himself bless you! You were inspired with a "bright idea"! You had one? Two? Many? Lucky breaks?

Don't rule out the positive possibility that God is alive and He blessed you with a dream, a determination, a discipline, a dedication to excel. That's where the "lucky breaks" came from.

You owe a lot to many—we all do.

Now comes the payoff!

Yes, the joy of saying "Thank you."

Patronize the sciences, the arts, the positive religious ministries, and discover the greatest achievement: to make a difference and make the world a more beautiful place.

I have the rare and rich position to know many, many philanthropists. What fabulous people. What happy people.

I am all for prosperity. John Wesley, founder of the Methodist denomination, said it so wisely and well: "Make all the money you can, save all the money you can, and give all the money you can."

Do you want an exciting new dream?

An impossible goal that can fill you with fresh motivational energy? Look at all of the great causes, ministries, projects in this world that need generous benefactors.

Okay, take your pick and decide to join the million-dollar club. These are persons who make gifts in the seven-figure bracket. What a fantastic club this is. One member I know has brought democracy to Russia by giving one million dollars every year to underwrite a weekly inspirational television program that reaches tens of millions, giving them the foundation of freedom. That program is "The Hour of Power." It has helped change history at the end of this century. Who does this? One patron whose gift alone makes this telecast possible. When the head of Russian television and the chief of President Boris Yeltsin's staff came to America, they called me and asked if I could set up an appointment for them and thank her. I did. I sat and heard the top power people from Moscow tell her that her philanthropy delivered the Power Thoughts that have empowered the people to believe in themselves and succeed as free men and free women in a competitive world.

She cried. With her one and only arm and hand she wiped the tears of joy from her cheeks.

You can be and you will be a patron, too.

Even if you're never superrich or superpowerful.

As you pursue your grand dreams, never forget the person you really want to be.

You want to be a success? Good. But why? Because

deep down in your heart you would enjoy being a generous philanthropist.

You can make your dreams come true and be proud of what you have achieved, the way in which you achieved it, and what you will do with what you have achieved.

Now, ask yourself, "What kind of person am I?" I have, in an earlier work, observed that there are three kinds of persons in this world.

ARE YOU AN I-I PERSON?

The I-I person finds emotional fulfillment in feeding an insecure ego, satisfying his selfish pleasures, and making sure he gets his own way. When faced with decisions, this kind of person asks questions like:

"What's in it for me?"

"What will I get out of it?"

"Does it fit in with my plans?"

No matter if others don't like it; no matter if others would be helped or not; no matter if others are hurting.

He is the nonsharing, noncaring, nonburden-bearing person.

Someone is crying? Tough!

Someone is dying? Rough!

"I've enough problems of my own" is his answer. Instead of "Please let me help you."

What kind of person are you?

Are you an I-I Person? or

ARE YOU AN I-IT PERSON?

Do you relate primarily to things? Do you find emotional fulfillment in things?

Want joy? Get something new.

Bored? Go out shopping.

Guilty? Buy a gift!

Fearful? Buy a gun!

Insecure? Build a bigger savings account.

Need to impress people? Cars, clubs, cocktails will do it.

Lonely? Go to a movie, a bar, or a motel!

Even people become things.

Not persons with hopes,

feelings,

dreams,

but instead they are

toys to play with,

tools to use,

trinkets for amusement,

treasures to buy, or

trash to throw away.

The I-It person will never be emotionally satisfied or fulfilled. You will find that things rust out, wear out, wrinkle, grow old or go out of style.

You probably never discover that things do not feed self-respect or self-esteem on any lasting basis.

I-It people ask different questions.

What's the salary?

What are the fringe benefits?

How much will it cost? These are the first questions.
I-It people are forever trapped by the tyranny of things.
Paint me,
plaster me,
patch me,
repair,
replace,
reupholster, or at least,
rearrange me.

ARE YOU AN I-YOU PERSON?

"I love you because I want you." This marks an I-I
person. "I love you because I need you" marks the love relationship of the I-It person. "I love you because you need me"
marks the I-You person.

What kind of person are you? In which category do
you think you fit at this stage of your life? I-I? or I-It? Can
you happily say, "I am an I-You person"? For then you relate
to other people who also have dreams, desires, hurts and
needs.

"I love you—because you need me!" That's real love.
And that's how I-You people relate. So I-You people love
people! They are the real success stories. They are the
patrons of the good and the beautiful!

WELCOME TO THE FIRST CLASS CLUB!

When an I-I person or an I-It person becomes an I-You
person, what a change takes place!

The housewife becomes a homemaker.

The sire becomes a father.

The lover becomes a husband.

The lawyer becomes a counselor.

The teacher becomes a person builder.

The doctor becomes a healer of the person.

The truck driver becomes a transporter of vital materials.

The salesman becomes a supplier of human need.

The businessman becomes a job-opportunity creator.

The capitalist becomes a builder of a better society through generating the money to create job opportunities!

You will become an I-You person, a patron of goodness and kindness, and holiness and helpfulness.

How? Through letting the love of God come into your daily life.

There are millions of human beings living on earth who have accepted Christ into their lives. They're able to love—unselfishly.

How can you become a person that you really like and like a lot?

How can you become ambitious, energetic, constructive and dynamic, really successful with a priceless personality of positive self-respect? By becoming an I-You person.

And you become an I-You person when you become an I-Him person.

BECOME AN "I-HIM" PERSON

Relate to Christ.

Whatever your faith or religion, you'll agree: What the

world needs is millions of beautiful people who love like Jesus loved!

Let his Spirit come into your personality.

You'll love people; you'll climb to the top and love yourself doing it.

Then you'll be a patron. That's Power Thinking and Power Sharing.

There was a man in Tennessee. Now this fellow was a wealthy, powerful and popular man in his town. Then he died. At his funeral there were many prestigious people from the political and business levels of society. As these people drove up the road to the cemetery, they saw a huge throng of people walking up the roadway. The sidewalks were so filled with people that many had to walk off the curb into the street.

A man in one of the limos wondered to himself, "Are all of these people coming to the funeral of Mr. Jones?" All the people that were walking were simple people and didn't look well-dressed. As they neared the front of the cemetery, the crowd thickened to where a police escort had to make way for the limousines.

Finally, the man's curiosity got the best of him. He poked his head out of the window and asked the officer, "Who are all of these people?"

"They are all here for the woman's funeral," the policeman told him.

The man in the limo was shocked. "What woman?" he asked. "Who could be so important? Who is she?"

"Did you pass the school on the way here?" the policeman asked the man.

"Yes, we did," the man answered.

"She was the crossing guard for twenty-nine years. These are the families of all the children she took care of all those years."

She discovered the best secret. So can you!

How to really live and move

FROM SUCCESS TO SIGNIFICANCE!

4

The Power
Within
the Power Thinkers

What sets these Power Thinkers apart?
They have connected with a profound, awesome
Power that activates, elevates and motivates!

─────────── 1 ───────────
POWER THINKERS HAVE "DREAMING"
POWER WITHIN.

"If you can dream it, you can do it!"

───────────────────────

That's power.
It's a power deep down
inside of you waiting to be turned on!
And it's high and holy power outside of you,

waiting to come in.
The human and the divine
have holy spiritual intercourse!
New life is being impregnated.
Creativity is in its divine spark of conception.
Before the scientist thinks.
Before the pastor prays,
before the researcher begins his mental probing,
there is:
THE DREAM!
Every human has the awesome capability of tapping
into this power.
To dream
To imagine
To fantasize
To mentally visualize
To create

SOMETHING OUT OF NOTHING!

The brain secretes its energetic chemicals.
There is conception!
The body comes alive with energy!
There's a holy hum.
In the turned-on thought processor!

Worlds whirl within whirling worlds
Orders are sent. Messages are transmitted.
Countless connections make their specialized contact.
Faster than the fastest speed ever imagined
Signals are sent, received, delivered and <u>executed</u>.

COMMUNICATION!
CATCH IT!
ENTHUSIASM!
EXCITEMENT!
ENERGY!

SPIRIT, MIND, BODY—all are working perfectly, beautifully, syncretistically, in an amazing exercise of harmonious productivity.

SOMETHING OUT OF NOTHING!

Nerves tingle. Muscles move. Energy surges.
Fantastic power is turned on!
Wow!
The power thought of a dream!
We are watching the power within the power thinker.
The spark is ignited in the eye.
There is fresh color in the skin! Cheeks lift!
Sculptured round and beautiful by a new excitement.
God has made a connection with one of His creatures.

Madrid, Spain, 1967. The World Psychiatric Congress is in session. I am there. Along with 4,000 delegates. The plenary speaker talks on "The Phenomenon of Hope."

This was his message as my memory system replays it years later.

The esteemed doctor of psychiatry is German. "Hope? What is it? We don't know," he said, continuing, "but we have all witnessed its marvelous and amazing healing powers."

The psychiatrist continues. "For months, we saw our

patients sit there. We tried to connect. We listened. We waited. We probed. But the face was gray, the eyes dull.

"No heart!

"Suddenly it happened! Life was turned on. Hope was born. Where did it come from?

"We, the professionals, don't know! What a magnificent mystery."

I call it the "phenomenon of hope." The doctor said, concluding, "We don't know where it came from, but what we do know is that suddenly there's life! Power!"

THE POWER WITHIN THE POWER THINKER IS THE POWER OF AN IDEA! IT'S THE ENERGY GENERATED BY A DYNAMIC DREAM!

I'll never forget the first time I preached in Moscow. It was in the pulpit of the First Baptist Church. This was years before the Cold War had ended. I was surprised to see it filled to overflowing, Even the aisles were jammed, but not because I was there. Sunday after Sunday this happened no matter who was preaching. I had prayed and prepared to deliver my single most important sermon that God had put within me.

My classic message on "How to Make Your Dreams Come True."

This is what some would call an "American Gospel," and here I was delivering it into the heart of a Communist empire. I was shocked to see old ladies in their babushkas nodding their heads up and down. And others were crying with tears running down their cheeks.

Yes. Of course, they dream, too. I didn't know what

their dreams were. Perhaps for health, maybe for food. Maybe the dream that their children would get a good education. Maybe that more people in this atheistic country would be able to hear the Good News that there is a God who loves and cares for his people

The exciting news is that there is an immense difference between your brain and the greatest computer that will ever be built in the centuries to come. There will never be a computer that has greater power and potential than exists in your brain today. For you have the capacity to dream,

AND IF YOU CAN DREAM IT, YOU CAN DO IT!

Every person, no matter where he or she lives, carries a dream deep within that's a source of power. You, too, have a dream inside of you. Tap into that power.

Never let a problem become an excuse for not dreaming beautiful dreams.

Never let a lack of anything become an excuse for not dreaming. For lacks can be compensated. You lack an education? You can compensate for that lack of education. Do you lack money? You can compensate for that. Compensation is the creative possibility. Dream dreams and dream bigger and more beautiful dreams.

Look at how the world has changed in just the last one hundred years. Automobiles. Jet airplanes. Telephones. Radio. Television. Computers. Great dreamers, thank you! God is a living God who is still creating by sending His exciting dreams into the minds of human beings who will be caught up, consumed and carried away as power-thinking dreamers! What Power!

"If you can dream it, you can do it." That really describes the authentic power thinker.

2

POWER THINKERS HAVE THE POWER WITHIN TO MANAGE WITH MAGNIFICENT ASSUMPTIONS.

"If you believe it, you can achieve it!"

I have had people proclaim that they "never make decisions on assumptions." And nothing could be more erroneous than that analysis.

Everybody manages from assumptions. What is an assumption? An old saying tells us never to assume, for when we leave the last three letters off the word—what's left of that word is what we become.

But the truth is we all make assumptions. We go to bed and we assume that we will awaken tomorrow. We sit in the chair without having the latest engineering report guaranteeing that the chair will not collapse.

We assume that the food we eat has not been infected with poison by somebody conspiring to kill us. Virtually every decision we make is based on assumptions.

Power Thinkers assume that their dream can come true. They assume it will produce problems and difficulties, but they assume that they can somehow protect themselves or immunize themselves from the difficulties.

They assume they can neutralize the impact that the difficulties could produce.

They calculate that the positives will outweigh the negatives so they move ahead.

MANAGEMENT BY ASSUMPTIONS POWER

This is living by what the Bible calls "faith." I operate with the magnificent assumption that my dreams are ideas put into my conscious computer from the Ultimate Command Center of Intelligent Thinking: <u>**God**</u>.

"I would love to be a believer if I knew it was the truth" an intelligent young Japanese student said to me as I finished my lecture in Tokyo. "Prove it to me," he challenged, adding, "That's what the unbelieving and skeptical world is waiting for. We're scientific. We're mathematical. We must have proof before we believe."

"But that's a contradiction," I replied. "If there is proof, there is no longer room for belief. For faith is believing in *that which cannot be proved.* Let me sum it up in this sentence:

WHEN PROOF IS POSSIBLE, FAITH BECOMES IMPOSSIBLE."

But, the young student continued, "If God wants us to live by faith, why didn't He prove himself to us?"

I quoted Hebrews 11:6, "Without faith it is impossible to please God." Explaining: "The same is true in human behavior and in social relations. When somebody believes in you before you have earned their trust you have been honored. When they trust you even when you didn't display the appropriate credentials, profound gratitude is born in your heart. Faith is born in that moment!"

God knew what he was doing when he established the

"belief" system. Strip away all mystery, leave all truth naked and mathematically and scientifically exposed, and something sweet and romantic will be removed.

"Twinkle, twinkle little star,
I know exactly what you are:
An incandescent ball of gas
Condensing to a solid mass."

There must always be the unknown. There must always be the unprovable. For faith confronts these frontiers with a thrilling leap and life becomes vibrant with adventure. Faith is dreaming God's dream.

What's the purpose of life anyway?

Only to eat, drink, work, play, make love?

Or do you have a brain designed to dream great dreams?

Is your mind created to be an architect? Drawing plans? Can you imagine beautiful accomplishments?

Think of this:

The human being is the only creature in the universe that has the capacity for exercising creative imagination.

This divine quality of <u>dreaming</u>

what you want to be,

where you want to go,

what you'd love to do,

projects you hope to achieve,

goals you'd like to reach—

all of this makes you human

and the most unique creature in all of creation!

You are designed to be the guardian to ecological architecture.

You really are "made in the image" of the Creator God!

So you are fulfilling your destiny as the child of God in human flesh.

When you start dreaming beautiful dreams,
God himself is inspiring in your mind.
A radio is designed to pick up the sounds
that are here in this room right now.

A television is engineered to pick up the moving pictures that are in the airwaves around you right now.

Your mind was invented and your spirit was created by God to pick up the messages and mental pictures he is sending your way this very moment.

That's exciting. Faith is the power within to manage with a magnificent assumption.

Faith is the mark of normality. A persistent negative, cynical doubt is not a mark of emotional health.

Birds were designed to fly.
The air under the wings of a bird
is the natural habitat of the flying fowl.
Water is the natural habitat of the fish.

Faith is the native air to humans. We're meant to breathe faith in and out to be healthy human spirits.

It is normal to have faith, it is abnormal to be cynical. Practice positive belief and you will be controlled by positive emotions: love, joy, humor, courage, aspiration, faith, affection, enthusiasm!

These are the marks of an emotionally healthy person. Persons who are not breathing the natural air of faith but are breathing the polluted air of doubt and unbelief and cynicism are quickly susceptible to a lower morality, and to an unacceptable level of ethical behavior. They are quickly consumed by negative emotions all of which are measured and marked as symptoms of something less than true wholeness and health as a human being.

You were created to be a believer.

Faith is finding your native air.

That's why you feel so fantastic when you are enthusiastic.

And faith is a choice, not an argument. It is a decision, not a debate.

It is a commitment, not a controversy.

Faith fulfills deep needs in your heart.

St. Augustine said it: "Our souls, O Lord, are restless till they rest in Thee."

We suspect that out there, somewhere, sometime, there is SOMETHING MORE. Where does this "intuition" for something more come from? It's built into our nature by the God who created us so that we would never be able to be excited and enthused and adventuresome until we were living and acting on causes that require faith. For faith means that there is something more that is going to happen to us. That means we could live optimistically without depression. Become a power thinker and you will reject the deep-seated negative emotions that would kill your desire to believe by letting you live under the negative inclinations to doubt.

But, Dr. Schuller, what if you come to the end of your life and someone told you, "It has now been discovered that all of your life you were wrong. There is no God. There is no afterlife. You blew it!" My answer? "I did not blow it. For it

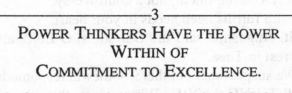

made me a better, nicer, more creative human being! I've lost nothing! If there is no God we must create one. And if we must create one make him like Jesus Christ—please."

You can't lose a thing if your faith in God is wrong. But all of life and whatever is beyond this life are really wasted if you closed all of your thinking and feeling to faith. I can't <u>lose</u> by choosing <u>to</u> believe—you could lose everything by choosing not to believe.

Choose to become a believer. Tap into believing power. Live like a power thinker. Decide to operate on magnificent assumptions.

3
POWER THINKERS HAVE THE POWER
WITHIN OF
COMMITMENT TO EXCELLENCE.

"Nothing great happens on the O.K. level."

You can see and spot this compulsion to excel in the personalities of Power Thinkers as soon as you meet them. Mediocrity commands little attention, and generates little energy and excitement. But Power Thinkers who are committed to excellence generate powerful enthusiasm.

I introduced you to a friend earlier who has the inner power of commitment to excellence, Power Thinker Herman Cain. He's the president and chief executive officer of Godfather's Pizza, Incorporated.

He's black. He was raised in poverty.

Now check his credentials. He graduated from Morehouse College with a bachelor of science in mathematics in 1967. He earned his master's degree in Computer Science from Purdue University in 1971.

Following employment with the navy and Coca-Cola, he joined the Pillsbury Company in 1977, rising to vice president of corporate systems and services in just five years. Sitting in his thirty-first-floor office and overlooking the great city of Minneapolis in 1982, Herman Cain was <u>bored</u> and decided to learn the hamburger business.

He left a top management position to start over again because he knew he'd missed valuable learning experiences. He started at the bottom and after only six months he became regional vice president with Burger King Corporation. He turned the Philadelphia region from the worst-performing region in Burger King's system to their best in less than three years. In 1986 he was selected by Pillsbury to assume the presidency of the failing Godfather's Pizza subsidiary, and turned the company to profitability in less than one year. Two years later, in 1988, he successfully led a select group of Godfather's Pizza senior management and negotiated the purchase of the pizza chain from the Pillsbury Company.

Herman Cain has received honorary doctorates from Morehouse College in Atlanta as well as from the University of Nebraska in Lincoln. He serves on many prestigious boards including the Federal Reserve Bank of Kansas City as vice chairman. He's married to a wonderful wife and he has a fabulous son and daughter.

I asked him, "Where did you get this inner drive just to be the best?"

"I believe it came from my father," he said. "My

father was a man who literally started with nothing and was able to make the most of his life. He was born on a farm in Tennessee, and yet he was eventually able to reach some of his dreams. The one thing I remember most about my father, as I was growing up, is that it didn't matter what it was that he was doing, whether it was working as a barber, working as a janitor, or working as a chauffeur, or whether it was cooking up one of his homemade batches of his homestyle barbecue ribs, he did everything with a zest and zeal and did it the best he could. He always had this attitude of positiveness and always enjoyed life and enjoyed people."

"So Herman, your father did not leave you a rich inheritance in terms of property, but he <u>did</u> leave you a rich inheritance of positive values!"

"That's right! We were short on possessions, we had just the bare essentials, in fact my brother and I had to sleep on a rollout bed in the kitchen. But it was a bed. Even so, by working three or four jobs at once, my father was able to save enough money to buy a house so his sons could have their own bedroom.

"He was so positive! He believed that you could not only get a job, but that if you worked hard enough and long enough, you could achieve whatever goals you set for yourself. And there was one other thing that my father believed that sticks with me to this day: There's no such thing as a bad job! <u>Every</u> job is a <u>good</u> job because it's where you start!"

Herman Cain's life history is organized around positive people. Listen to him. "In addition to the inspiration that I got from my mother and my father, I was also inspired by two of my high school teachers who took an interest in me. In their own way at various times, other than in the classroom, they said, 'Herman, you are somebody and you can be whoever you want to be and you can achieve whatever you want to achieve.'

"I specifically remember my math teacher, who was my math teacher all the way through high school, Mr. Johnson, who said, 'You may not have the best high school background, you may not even have the best college background; but if you work just a little bit harder than the next guy, you can go just as far.' And I never did forget that."

"Hermain Cain," I asked, "some people are very negative. They're poor. They probably don't have a bedroom or a bed to sleep in. They're victims of prejudice, racial, religious, political or cultural. It's very hard for them to believe that they can make it like you made it."

"Give them some Power Thoughts so they can succeed, too.

"What comes to my mind is first, belief. Belief in Christ and in yourself. When I was attending Morehouse College, our president at that time was Dr. Benjamin Elijah Mays, and he would always use a poem from time to time that to this day I can never forget. This poem helps to encourage me in my life, not only in business but personally. Here it is:

"Life is just a minute
Only sixty seconds in it,
Forced upon you, can't refuse it.
Didn't seek it, didn't choose it,
But it's up to you to use it.
You must suffer if you lose it,

Give an account if you abuse it,
Just a tiny little minute,
But eternity is in it."

Herman Cain's testimony is similar to mine. I have always been driven by an incurable compulsion for excellence. And for me it is a spiritual motivation. I believe that my dreams have come from God. I believe they are His dreams for this world. I believe He has chosen to use me to materialize His dream in humanity. And I have a stewardship, that means RESPONSIBILITY, to manage His dream and materialize that dream in an achievement that I can return to Him without spot, wrinkle or imperfection.

And with honest commitment I say to God, "Father, here's your idea, I've carried it out. I'm proud of what I have done and how you've made it possible for me not to fail you!"

Then in my mind I imagine a God of Love who deserves to be worshipped, honored and adored receives the best gift I can give to Him. His dream is returned to Him in the form of an achievement that really has helped and healed a hurting person.

That commitment to excellence gives me the power to do what God wants me to do with the one life I have.

———————————— 4 ————————————
THE POWER THINKER HAS IMPROVING POWER WITHIN.

"If it works, improve it!"

The Power Thinker is driven by a power drive deep within that I call "Compulsive Improvement Complex."

Power Thinkers are always trying to improve and perfect what they are selling.

Recently I had the pleasure of arranging a luncheon where I could introduce two of my friends to meet each other for the first time: Yukiyafu Togo, chairman, Toyota Motor Sales, U.S.A., Inc., and Louis Sullivan, a newly elected director of General Motors, Detroit, Michigan, who for four years was a member of President George Bush's cabinet. Now Dr. Sullivan would meet Mr. Togo, "Mr. Toyota of North America." When I was starting a church from scratch more than thirty years ago, this young Japanese came to North America to see if he could get Americans conceivably to buy a car not made in Detroit, Michigan. He asked thousands of them, "What would you like in a car? How could we make it better?" Back in California a young minister was asking, "What would you like in a church? How could we make it better?" Both Togo and I were empowered with a "Compulsive Improvement Complex." Mr. Togo's last project was the Lexus—winning the 1993 Car of the Year Award. Mr. Togo agreed most generously to host the luncheon in his corporate office.

"I want to give to both of you a gift," I offered. "If

117

both Toyota and General Motors accept it—live by it, <u>think with it</u>—then <u>everyone in the world</u> will benefit!

"First let me tell you it's a new slogan. For nearly 20 years I had a friend whom I've admired, respected and listened to. Now I realize this friend has betrayed me! I've broken off our relationship. And I've replaced the rejected 'friend' with a real friend. The 'friend' I've rejected after twenty years of love is a bumper sticker:—'If it works, don't fix it!'"

I suspect General Motors was in love with the same slogan. But in a free world market, people will see what works. They'll want "a piece of the action." Ambitious competitors will use innovative skills to improve the product, allowing them to win a portion of the large market. So if you want your success to continue, then you need to replace the slogan.

The old expression is:

> ~~If it works, don't fix it.~~

Now, here's my new Power Thought:

> *If it works . . . improve it!*

Yes—if it works, improve it or someone else will! Success that has happened or is happening is never certain.

Some years ago I was invited by the University of California in Irvine to lecture for several hours to the top corporate leaders in the state of California. All were supersuccessful. Many were CEOs of billion-dollar corporations. For three hours I talked on this sentence that I wrote on the white board:

"IF THERE'S A MARKET
FOR YOUR PRODUCT OR SERVICE
AND YOU'RE HAVING PROBLEMS
FIRST—check manufacturing
THEN—check marketing
NEXT—check merchandising
And if you still have troubles—

IT'S GOT TO BE IN MANAGEMENT."

So Power thinkers "invent change" that will bring improvement. Negative thinkers, psychologists tell us, perceive change as loss. Power Thinkers plan change, make changes, to improve the best!

Power Thinkers carefully research into every potentially positive idea by asking sensible questions like: Who needs it? Can we do it better, faster or cheaper than anybody else? Critical questions are asked. The success potential is studied carefully.

Moral and ethical judgments, of course, have to be asked before the Power Thinker invests his energy, his emotion, his wealth, his credentials, his reputation to an effort.

If there is some honest and authentic improvement

119

possible the Power Thinker never votes no. He will say:

> Yes—if:
> Yes—when:
> Yes—but:
> Yes—after:
> Yes—with:
> Yes—however:

The esteemed research psychologist Martin Seligman, Ph.D., is someone I have admired for many years. In his marvelous book *Learned Optimism* he makes this powerful and profound announcement. "Every person has one word in his heart. It is either a 'yes' or a 'no.'"

Power Thinkers are the people that go through life with a "yes" in their hearts.

No wonder the Power Thinker uses his power to choose his reactions positively! He deliberately rejects negative reactions. His optimism wins again!

5

POWER THINKERS HAVE PLANNING POWER.
THIS MAKES THEM DYNAMIC OPTIMISTS.

"If you fail to plan, you're planning to fail."

The Power Thinker is constantly motivated to manage his future by making smart decisions.

He's constantly driven to shape his destiny by setting divinely inspired goals.

Then he lets his goals motivate him! Manage him! Manipulate him!

If God birthed his dream and encouraged his goal-setting, then God remains in charge as long as <u>goals are in command</u>.

So his God, through His goals, not his own personal desires, <u>manages his behavior</u>. The question he asks is: Will what I'm doing today help me reach my goal? He surrenders leadership of his dreams to the goals he has set prayerfully and carefully—and darefully.

Only yesterday I was asked, "Why are you always up, Dr. Schuller? Don't you ever have a bad day or a bad week? I've had an awful week." The question was addressed to me by a wonderful young man who was giving me a radio interview prior to my going to Missouri to encourage the people who were the victims of the great flood of 1993.

My answer was quite predictable. "Am I always up? I guess I'm almost always up. Because my mind is occupied by what I'm going to do tonight or tomorrow—and guess what? Not a single trouble or problem has happened <u>there</u> yet. I'm only planning and preparing for good things to happen, not bad things. All of the goals and decisions I make and I'm working on, I'm enthused about. That's my tonight and tomorrow. And I'll succeed—a little? Or a <u>lot</u>!"

I don't know what <u>all</u> will happen tonight or tomorrow or next year, but I do know <u>a lot of what will happen</u>. For I have set goals, I have written letters, I have made telephone calls, I have contacted a lot of people, and I will get letters and calls and contacts back. And all of that will amount to a lot of good for me.

For I have prayerfully made what I'm sure are wise decisions,

121

I have laid beautiful plans,

I am pursuing some exciting dreams,

And all of my decisions, goals and plans are designed for good things to happen in my life by making good things happen in the lives of other people.

I cannot totally fail.

I may not completely succeed.

But good things are inevitable in my tomorrows because I have made decisions today that will cause reactions to come to me from many people and places that will be good. So negative experiences, or bad experiences I may have had earlier today, yesterday, or this past week, are not in my active consciousness. These "unpleasant" or "negative" or "bad" experiences are overwhelmed by my present positive expectations and optimistic predictions of what's going to happen tonight and tomorrow!

Plan good things and you can expect something good to happen to you.

"So you had trouble," I said to my radio interviewer, "you had a bad week? Thank God, for this is <u>past tense</u>! It happened. Now set goals, make plans, commit yourself to decisions that will correct, resurrect or sublimate the negative experience. Make exciting, good and beautiful plans for tonight, tomorrow and the next year and the next year."

The single most significant power that you and I have is to be able to shut doors that should not remain open and open doors that should not remain locked.

If we do not open them and walk through them nobody is going to open them for us and we'll miss out on a happy tomorrow.

I shut the door on yesterday
and threw the key away.

Tomorrow has no fears for me,
for I have found today.

Yes, today is the day I will make the plans that will bring me good experiences tomorrow!

6

THE POWER THINKER HAS THE POWER WITHIN OF LIBERATED THINKING.

"I'm not free 'til I believe in me."

The Power Thinker is a liberated person.

How liberated are you?

Liberated from fear of failure?

Liberated from inferiority complexes?

Liberated from worries about the future?

Liberated from internal insecurity?

Liberated from your dependence on "society" and "institutions" and "political power structures"?

We are not free until we are truly self-confident persons. Only a strong self-confidence will liberate you from surrendering to intimidation or manipulation.

A person is not free because he's offered food, clothing and medical care. This is not in itself the pathway to internal security. In fact, this "free food" may deepen your enslavement to a dependence on others.

123

Only the person who has a profound internal security, called self-confidence or self-esteem, is truly "free."

Without this power of self-esteem within us, we become the serfs or the subjects of patrimonious powers. Perhaps it's a political power, perhaps it's a religious control. Perhaps it's an internal psychological oppression.

Power Thinkers who practice liberated thinking have the power of freedom to dream dreams and to achieve the fulfillment of their dreams before they die.

7

NOW THE POWER THINKER HAS THE INNER POWER TO BE CREATIVE.

"If I can 'see it,' I can 'be it.'"

Power thinkers somehow tap into the power of creativity.

Where does this amazing power to be creative come from? We don't always know. And that can be frustrating.

My dear friend Roger Williams is known worldwide as "Mr. Piano." He has performed before the great people of the world. He is often invited to the dressing rooms of other great artists who perform on stage. He has a collection of experiences that are impressive. He tells this story:

One night, Laurence Olivier, one of the greatest actors of all time gave his most brilliant, never-to-be-matched performance onstage. The audience gave curtain call after curtain call after curtain call. Olivier retreated to his dressing room, locked the door, and from the hallway he could be heard screaming in his private place. The producer, alarmed, knocked on the door, opened it, stepped in and saw the actor "tearing his hair out."

"What's wrong?! You were at your incredible best! You were a genius in your creative performance tonight," the producer said. "You have never been that good." With a pitiful, pained, pathetic look the great master performer answered in a soft, defeated whisper, "Yes, you are right. But what infuriates me is—I don't know why."

Where does this mysterious, marvelous, creative power come from? Could it be "God working within us"? Surely exciting dreams, visions, creative imagination are part of a system God uses to help us discover and develop our "gifts," our "skills," our "talents."

When you are truly free, you can begin to see "the possible person that you can be."

We are designed to be "imagining" persons.

Imagination! What a power! There it is!

We have the power to be creative, and to design in our minds fabulous fantasies that can materialize into fruitful and fulfilling forms.

Fantastic fantasies. Call them power thoughts!

We may not know why, we may not understand how, but we simply allow the God who created us to stimulate, activate, motivate and replicate this power thinking called dynamic creativity.

Grab hold of this power!

—— 8 ——

POWER THINKERS HAVE THE POWER
OF AFFIRMATIVE THINKING.

"I am, therefore I can!"

---

1. Power Thinkers tap into the power of affirmative thinking, for affirmative thinking is "empowered thinking."

2. When I really empower you, I'll surely empower myself too!

I feel great when I make people feel great!

3. I must build the self-esteem of everyone I connect with. This motive drives the Power Thinker. Power Thinkers intuitively or intelligently know that a healthy self-esteem is the single most profound psychological need of every human being. I remember asking the world-famed psychologist Dr. Victor Frankl from the University of Vienna a question. After one of his lectures I met him in the hallway outside the classroom and I said, "Now, Dr. Frankl, can you summarize for me the history of psychological theory?"

"Well," he answered, "Sigmund Freud assumed it was 'will to pleasure.' That's the one thing all human beings need and if they don't have it they are going to become emotionally and probably mentally ill.

"To Adler it was the 'will to power.' Power, he said, is more important to a person than pleasure. If you don't have power, you'll feel you can't cope.

"To me, it's 'will to meaning,'" he said. "I can deal without pleasure and I can deal without power, but I cannot deal without meaning." He came to that conclusion when, as a Jew, he was sentenced to a concentration camp during World War II.

Then I asked Dr. Frankl, "Why? Why is meaning so important? And why is power so important to others, and why is pleasure so important to so many others?"

His answer was short and simple: "I don't know."

That would send me on a track of study which brought me three years later to a stimulating three-hour visit with Dr. Victor Frankl again in my office at the Crystal Cathedral.

"Have you discovered why meaning, power and pleasure are so important to persons?"

His answer: "No, I have not."

"I have," I boldly declared.

He looked a bit shocked at my apparent lack of humility, but listened. "I have discovered something more important than pleasure, power and meaning," I answered. "It is dignity. The will to self-esteem, call it the will to self-dignity, call it the will to self-love, call it the will to be treated with a touch of glory and honor, call it what you want to, but that's what we all need." (1) No person wants to be humiliated, or ashamed. (2) We all want to maintain our dignity. (3) That's why we all need the power of healthy, humble pride. (4) Humble pride is not a contradiction. It is a precious paradox.

FOR THE OPPOSITE OF PRIDE IS NOT HUMILITY. THE OPPOSITE OF PRIDE IS SHAME, EMBARRASSMENT OR HUMILIATION. We do not want to be manipulated, coerced or intimidated into doing and being something other than what God wants us to be. We don't want to be embarrassed, humiliated, disrespected. We want to be respected.

The power of affirmative thinking: That's what motivates Power Thinkers to build self-esteem in people and in the process build it in themselves!

So Power Thinkers are great encouragers.

They are affirmative persons!

They empower people at the deepest taproot of the human personality.

9

POWER THINKERS HAVE THE POWER OF PERSISTENCE.

"Tough times never last, but tough people do!"

Power Thinkers need power of persistence. Where does it come from?

I can say with absolute honesty that I have wanted to walk away, give up and quit, more than a dozen times in my career.

Why haven't I?

What gave me the power of persistence?

For years I have had under the glass top of my desk a little clipping that I cut out of a magazine somewhere decades ago. It was a quote attributed to Dr. Butler, professor of English at Baylor University in Texas. Here's the quote; I know it from memory: "When things get tough don't move. People and pressures shift but the soil remains the same no matter where you go."

This is the Power Thought that became the title of one of my books:

"Tough times never last, but tough people do." I began that book with this simple prayer:

Lord,
give me the guidance
to know
when to hold on
and
when to let go
and the grace
to make the right decision
with dignity.

By the grace of God, that's the power within the Power Thinker. It's faith (Positive Thinking).

It's focused faith (that's Possibility Thinking).

It's follow-through faith (that's Power Thinking).

I attribute my internal power of persistence to an internal spirit that is at the heart of my personality. It is the presence of Jesus Christ who lives in my life and whom I hold as my Lord and my Savior. It is the presence of God within me.

My colleagues who have worked beside me for years and years tell me it is my "persistence" that keeps me from quitting. That could well be. For more years than I can recall, I also kept another saying under the glass top of my desk, a Bible verse. The words of Jesus Christ: "No man having put his hand to the plow and looking back is fit for the Kingdom of God." (Luke 9:62)

When the Power within the Power Thinker comes from God, the Power Thinker never quits!

10

THE POWER THINKER BELIEVES IN THE GREATEST POWER WITHIN.

"If there's a will, we'll find a way."

What is this Greatest Power within? Let's review the powers within the Power Thinker.
1. Dreaming power
2. Believing power
3. Winning power
4. Improving power
5. Planning power
6. Liberating power
7. Creative power
8. Affirming power
9. Persisting power

All of this adds up to the presence of God within you! Reread all nine points above, and you can see how God motivates, moves and masterfully manages people! All this points to

10. The Greatest Power. This is the power of the presence of God within you! The Master Programmer is at work in the computer called YOU. It is God the Cosmic Programmer fueling, feeding the alive and alert power thought processor—YOU.

Power Thinker Michelle Hamilton from Australia grabbed hold of the Greatest Power within. I was riveted as she recently shared her story at the Crystal Cathedral from her book, *A Mighty Tempest*.

"What started off as a relaxing holiday on a tropical island in the Philippines 950 miles south of Manila called Borokay suddenly turned into an ordeal. I had been holidaying there with my mother. We'd been there about four days when we decided to travel around to the other side of the island. We took out what was known as a 'bunker,' which is a seven-foot canoe with two outriggers on the side. This tiny vessel is so narrow you cannot actually sit in it.

"The boat began taking water right from the start, and my mother, who was bailing, said, 'I'm getting terrified. Take me to shore.' I dropped her back on shore and then took off by myself. At this point I was safe in the tranquil lagoon waters. But when I tried to get around to the other side of the island, the ocean currents from behind swept me straight out to sea. At about 5:30 p.m. storm clouds were brewing and suddenly I heard this peal of thunder and lightning streaked across the sky, illuminating massive waves that crashed over my bunker. I was in the middle of the most ferocious tropical storm. All I could do was wedge myself sideways in the canoe and hang on as the boat rode up onto the crest of these waves and them plummeted to the very depths. Every minute I thought I would die.

"I managed somehow to survive the night, but the next morning the boat capsized and I spent the next forty-eight hours up to my neck in the South China Sea in shark-infested waters, hanging on with one arm wrapped around one of the

outriggers which had broken off in the storm. I didn't feel I could possibly survive for long. I was bleeding into the water, which obviously attracted the sharks, and suddenly I saw them right in front of me. I was so gripped with fear that it was like somebody had reached inside my heart and was there squeezing, squeezing, squeezing it!

"I quickly threw myself onto the overturned bunker, but that was a mistake because it was covered with a slimy green algae. I was lying on it on my stomach, when suddenly a wave swept me from behind like a torpedo—right into the path of these sharks. When I surfaced they were ten to fifteen meters right in front of me. My fear was so intense. Somehow I found myself swimming back to the boat, all the while telling myself, 'Don't splash . . . don't splash . . . Just then I heard a Voice saying, 'Do not fear, for they will not hurt you.'

"Nobody was there. I was alone. Who was talking to me? I have no doubt it was the voice of God telling me, 'Do not fear, for they will not hurt you.'

"I truly believe that God snatched me from the jaws of death! The sharks left me alone and I continued to scan the skies for help. I continually looked into the sky, expecting to be rescued any minute. I hoped against hope to see a plane or a helicopter—but nothing came. On the second evening as the sun began to fade, I realized I would have to spend another freezing night—lost, alone in that cold water. Once more I called out to God.

"I wanted to know. So I asked Him, '<u>Am I going to die?</u>'

"To tell you the truth, I didn't expect to get an answer

but this very powerful, audible voice burned down from the Heavens, calling out, 'No! You are not going to die!' It was a Voice that went right through my body as well as through my ears. It was as if every particle of my body recognized that <u>this was the voice of God</u>!

"I was in such awe I couldn't believe that He said that. I said, 'Can you say it again?' And the Voice came clearly, 'No, you are not going to die!' I asked Him, 'What do you want from me in return?' He called out, 'I want 100 percent of your faith.'

"I wasn't a Christian. I didn't know what faith was. It was this next statement that made me realize that God knew what I was thinking before I even thought it.

"He said, 'Not 90 percent faith, I said <u>100 percent faith</u>.'

"Even though I was not a Christian, I cried out to God because I was <u>powerless</u> to save myself. I had American Express on me, I had all this money in my money belt, but it couldn't save me. <u>Only God had the power to spare my life.</u>

"My rescue was an amazing feat. A fishing boat came very near me, but it continued on for almost a mile before finally somebody on the boat spotted me.

"Rescue! Not quite! I still had to swim through the shark-infested waters to the side of the boat. Then I collapsed into unconsciousness. I was saved <u>physically</u> and <u>spiritually</u> by the Power of a Living God. Today I have the Super Power within! I call him <u>JESUS</u>!"

Now you know how the Super Power Thinkers are empowered. Become one! Become a believer! When the greatest power empowers the Power Thinker, then the greatest problems of the next century are solvable.

Power Thinker, welcome to the hall where heroes march!

Power Thinker, welcome to the twenty-first century!

Power Thinker, your time has come!

5

How Power Thinkers Handle Power Thoughts!

Earlier this year, I attended the most astounding conference of my life. I was invited to be a member of the American Academy of Achievement. My invitation letter was signed by three members: Oprah Winfrey, Richard De Vos, and Philip Johnson. The conference was attended by such people as General Norman Schwarzkopf, Tom Selleck, Wynonna Judd and Johnny Cash. The new members included Nobel Prize winners in physics and math, Pulitzer Prize–winning authors, supersuccessful corporate CEOs, famous medical researchers and entertainers. Almost every imaginable profession and career were represented.

I've never attended a conference like it. Day after day,

I listened to speaker after speaker, dozens of them! Each shared their secrets of successful achievement. I took careful notes, interfaced their testimonies with lessons I've learned and have shared in thirty books and 1,250 telecast messages, and here is my up-to-date summary!

Power Thinkers who have managed to succeed do so because they know how to handle the Power Thoughts that come swiftly, silently, unexpectedly into their minds.

Let me summarize, in my own words, how I see the way Power Thinkers handle Power Thoughts:

—————— 1 ——————

"SEIZE YOUR MOMENT."

In the words of Betty Condon, "Be ready when the moment comes," and "Be the best audience possible."

I would add:

> "Opportunity is when a prepared person
> sees a need."
> "Preparation comes to those who know
> how to listen to advice."
> "I'm not ego-involved—I'm success-oriented."
> "I don't want my own way—I don't
> want to make mistakes."

When I was five years old, my uncle, a Princeton Theological Seminary graduate, returned from China, saw me and said, "So you're Robert. You'll be a minister when you grow up." I listened to that Power Thought. I had my life's call! My goal was set.

Sixteen years later, when I was twenty-one—soon to graduate from theological seminary—a lecturer in seminary said, "My advice is, never accept a job in a church unless you can envision spending your life there." Another Power Thought! I believed it, so I welcomed the chance to go to California at the age of twenty-eight to start a brand new church, and determined to commit forty years to that goal.

At the age of twenty-two I met a girl named Arvella De Haan. I had one date with her, and recalled a comment by my undergraduate psychology professor: "When you get ready to look for a wife, use your head and your heart will follow." This is a fabulous Power Thought that was meant for me. The morning after my first date with Arvella I wrote my best friend a letter: "I've met the girl I'm going to marry."

Four years later, married and an ordained minister in the Reformed Church of America, I was riding on the train, returning from a trip to check out whether I would really decide to accept the California invitation to start a new church in that far-off state. The train stopped suddenly at midnight somewhere in the snow-capped mountains of Arizona. I jolted awake. Outside I saw a vast space of deep snow covering pine trees in a totally desolate wilderness lighted in a full midnight moon. Suddenly from behind a tree blanketed with soft, thick snow right outside my window, I saw a large deer bound forward. Antlered head held proudly high, white tail reflecting white moonlight. He jumped, leaped, bounced, disappeared—leaving black holes where his feet had landed. In that still, quiet, serene moment a POWER

THOUGHT shot into my brain. Strange! I had fallen asleep praying for divine guidance. I was prepared to receive God's message. Now he sent to me this promise: "The greatest churches in the world have yet to be organized."

I listened, I heard the Power Thought! I believed. I accepted the call. I found my gift called Guidance. A month later, with $500, my wife and two small children, including a four-month-old baby boy, Robert A. Schuller, we arrived in California.

How do you handle POWER THOUGHTS?
Be prepared to welcome them when they come.
Beverly Masek is a Power Thinker!

Beverly Masek is an Alaskan Native American who was born and raised in Anvik, a very small village in the interior of Alaska with a population of about seventy people. The most noise you'll ever hear in Anvik is during the Iditarod when the church bells welcome each musher into town. The Iditarod is a dog-sled race where one person runs all alone, through blizzards, for 1,029 miles! It's the most astounding race to test a solitary human's courage and strength.

In 1977 something else greeted mushers here. A twelve-year-old girl who came to listen to some stories about life on the trails came away with something more—a lifelong ambition to run the Iditarod.

Beverly Masek was that twelve-year-old girl who had the determination to pursue her dream.

When Beverly saw the dog sleds come through she said, "Someday I'm going do that." She said that even though she didn't own one dog or sled. All she had was a dream.

She'd see the teams leaving the village and each time they'd ring the bell for every musher. Whether it was one in the morning or five in the morning, there was someone there to greet each musher. And Beverly just thought, "Someday I'd like to hear the bell ring for me." Now they ring the bell when Beverly comes through, no matter what time of the day or night. Beverly has completed the Iditarod run four times!

The racer is all alone with no other human being. Just the dog team. She gets help from no one. She has to provide for herself as well as the dogs. Beverly told me, "I have to feed the dogs. I lift the dogs [seventy or eighty pounds] and I weigh only one hundred pounds. You have to be able to take care of the dogs and provide for them year-round, it's a commitment of many years. I'm in my eighth generation of breeding my own dogs. Sometimes we run into an icy trail or fresh snow and sometimes it's about forty degrees below zero out there and I still have to take care of the dogs. There are times when I feel like I don't know if I can continue but I have to trust the Lord to help me because every mile, as we get farther into the race, I get more tired and have to rely on my dogs completely. But then again there always is that shining light at the end when I focus on reaching my goal."

Beverly's goals and dreams are accomplishing great things in her life. She wants to be a patron to children, so she travels to the schools to deliver messages of setting goals and achievement and tries to inspire excellence. As Beverly said, "When I grew up, I didn't have too many positive role models coming to motivate me. I have to do everything on my own out there on the Iditarod. When I tell the children in the schools that I compete in this thousand-mile race, they are all so surprised. They look at me and say, 'You actually finish this race?'

"That's why I continue to do it, to just inspire and show people that you don't have to be large, or great, if you choose a goal in life and you work hard.'"

2

"MAKE DUST—DON'T RUST."

I grew up on an Iowa farm. Few if any of the roads were paved. To this day, the roads that crisscross the countryside are gravel—and very dusty! I always hated it when I had to follow another car on those dusty roads! The dust would billow in through the windows and catch in our throats. How much better it was to be the leader, to be in front, making the dust, rather than following someone else and eating someone else's dust!

My friend J. B. Hunt, America's most successful trucking corporate leader, advised, "Don't waste time after you know what you want to be, where you want to go, whatever you want to accomplish. Make dust—or eat it," he challenged.

Every person has a God-given gift. Find yours. This is your calling! This is your destiny. This is how to make dust!

You long for it, dream of it, thirst for it!

You'll thank God it's Monday.

Friday may not be your most exciting day.

Get going! Just do it! Don't surrender the leadership

of your dream to fears of failure. Believe in your bliss and kiss it! And go! Make some dust!

My friends Naomi and Wynonna Judd, mother and daughter, were a most fantastic singing duet. Then Naomi fell ill and had to quit. What would Wynonna do? She worried. Meanwhile, Wynonna prayed: "How can I go on without Mom?"

Her answer? "Follow your gift." She grabbed hold of this Power Thought and said to herself, "I am! I can! I will follow my bliss." She wasted no time! Immediately she made commitments to make it on her own—alone with her faith. She made her own music—she made her own dust!

Seize the moment. The window of opportunity is like a satellite passing overhead. Only a few hours and it will leave my home in the dark and it will be on the other side of the globe! "Do it now" is the impulsive urgency of top achievers.

Make dust—don't rust!

This doesn't mean reckless pursuit with ill preparation. "Measure three times but cut only once" is another Power Thought from a Russian tailor that you can use here. Know where you're going before you make dust!

"What's the secret of my success?" a general was asked. He answered, "I decided I would always be the firstest with the mostest. I always was the first with the most . . . and I never lost a battle."

What have you done yesterday? What can you do today? What will you do tomorrow to make dust? Power Thinkers don't just sit on their dreams. They handle their power thoughts by seizing them—NOW!

————————— 3 —————————

"BEGINNING IS HALF DONE."

That Power Thought motivated me to find a drive-in theater where I could start a church without any money! I wasted no time. I made that connection six days after I arrived in the state of California.

"Beginning is half done." That Power Thought motivated me to slip a page of clean white paper in my typewriter. I typed the title of my first major book, *Move Ahead with Possibility Thinking*. One amazing Power Thought motivated me to get started. I licked my biggest problem: inertia!

————————— 4 —————————

"I'D RATHER ATTEMPT TO DO SOMETHING GREAT AND FAIL THAN ATTEMPT TO DO NOTHING AND SUCCEED."

Fear of failure has kept more people from running with their power thoughts. "What if I try and fail? What will people say?" Power Thinkers have had to work through this tough business of emotionally handling risk . . . and there is risk in every Power Thought!

If it's easy—everybody is there.

If it's safe—you'll find a big crowd.

If it's hard or risky, you'll find little or probably no competition.

One of the members of my corporate board of directors is Dr. Buert Ser Vaas. For thirty years he has been president of the City Council of Indianapolis, Indiana, and has made that city renowned and respected in education, medical advancements, athletics and business.

He himself is a supersuccess. I attribute my next Power Thought to him:

5

"DARE TO GO WHERE NO ONE ELSE HAS GONE."

In the summer 1993 edition of the magazine <u>Possibilities</u>, we shared the true story of how one brave boy and his family were fighting to cure a dreadful disease.

Viewers of the recent movie <u>Lorenzo's Oil</u> watched in horror as an ordinary, middle-class couple encountered every parent's worst nightmare—a terminal diagnosis for their only child. But when the doctors pronounced a death sentence on Lorenzo Odone, his parents refused to accept the verdict of conventional medical wisdom.

Michaela and Augusto's five-year-old son suffered a rare, metabolic disorder that was literally destroying his brain. The doctors told them, "Disease will steadily rob his movement, his sight, his hearing and his consciousness."

Death would snatch their only child within two years, the experts predicted. There was no treatment, no therapy, no hope. No child had ever survived this heartless disease for more than two years.

143

But the experts didn't count on the miracle the Odones would call down from heaven—a miracle born of devotion so strong that it transformed two parents with little scientific background into world-renowned experts on this rare disease and led them to invent its only known therapy, a cooking oil they named after Lorenzo.

Theirs is the miracle of love—a stubborn love that simply refused to let Lorenzo go.

"The love of a child is an extraordinary inspiration for anyone to get up, think positively and do something," Michaela says. "How could we not believe in Jesus when we'd been given a gift like Lorenzo? We would trivialize his whole life if we didn't."

The experts told the Odones that this extremely rapid, degenerative disease would soon completely destroy the white matter of Lorenzo's brain. They were to go home, make him comfortable and wait for the end. "They made it clear to us there was nothing anyone could do," Michaela says. "That was probably the most devastating piece of news any parent could be given."

Upon hearing the diagnosis, Augusto asked a resident doctor at the hospital for written materials about the condition. He was soundly reprimanded: "Oh, I wouldn't bother," said the doctor. "You wouldn't be able to understand them anyway."

But "not to bother" was not part of the Odones' natures. Ignoring the bleak prognosis and condescending advice, they plunged into educating themselves about this little-known disease. Their house in Washington, D.C., was less than a mile from the world's greatest medical library, housed at the

National Institutes of Health in Bethesda, Maryland. The day after the diagnosis, Augusto sequestered himself there, studying stacks of publications he culled from the *Index Medicus.*

What he learned broke his heart. The disease, adrenoleukodystrophy, more commonly referred to as ALD, strikes only boys between ages five and twelve. This disease with a very long name is essentially a disorder of very long fat molecules, known as very-long-chain-saturated fatty acids (VLCFAs).

A buildup of these fatty acids damages the membrane protecting each nerve cell in the brain and spinal cord. This membrane, called "myelin," insulates the nerve fibers in much the same way as a plastic sheath insulates electrical wire. Myelin protects the passage of nerve impuses from one part of the body to another. When this sheath is damaged, as by ALD, progressive disability leads to death.

Because of Lorenzo's condition, certain enzymes in his body were unable to break down the VLCFAs. Fats that would normally be dispersed had accumulated in his brain. This buildup triggered an immune reaction, and the immune system itself attacked the myelin around Lorenzo's nerve fibers.

Without that protection, his nerves were unable to communicate, and Lorenzo's bodily functions began breaking down. Already the gifted lad who had mastered English, Italian, and French; read voraciously from Greek mythology; and thrived on Italian Baroque music—all before his fifth birthday—was losing his hearing. Daily his speech grew more slurred, his gait more unsteady, and his once impeccable behavior more disruptive.

The Odones faced a terrible decision: Would they leave Lorenzo to fate? Or would they attempt the impossible—try to find a cure, something the experts said couldn't be done.

The answer was immediate: Love was stronger than death.

"Yes, we accepted that Lorenzo had this disease," says Michaela. "But were we going to sit on our hands and do nothing? No, never for a second!

"To just let him go was unthinkable for us," she adds. "We came to believe that God chose us to help find a cure. As painful as it was, we accepted that the hand of God put us on this path. When I asked Lorenzo if he was that SURE Jesus chose him, he said 'yes' with his hands.

"I wish God had not involved Lorenzo, but he did. Probably because, in His infinite wisdom, God knew that Augusto and I would not have devoted ourselves so ferociously to this cause had our son's life not been at stake."

So began the race against time. The Odones' odyssey unfolded like a mystery novel. Their mission was to track down the "bad guys," the VLCFAs, and destroy them before they destroyed Lorenzo. Augusto, an economist with the World Bank, spent every available minute researching. Michaela's family helped with Lorenzo—who required more care as his balance and coordination deteriorated—so she could also study.

"A lot of naysayers tried to discourage us," remembers Michaela. "Doctors and researchers didn't want to talk to us because we were only lay people. But we started with the basics and educated ourselves on this highly scientific subject. We learned the language of doctors so they would talk to us."

The Odones found that God's grace was sufficient to overcome this daunting task. "We turned our house into a sort of cramming factory, studying how the disease operated," says Michaela. "As co-creators with God of Lorenzo's life, we could do no less.

"Dr. Schuller called to encourage us," she says. "It was truly a gift of God to hear his voice on the telephone telling us to ignore the naysayers and keep on with our mission.

"Every Sunday, week after week, we never missed Dr. Schuller's 'Hour of Power.' We couldn't have kept up without this Possibility Thinking," she reported.

The couple became familiar fixtures at the medical library. They waded through huge stacks of research, found a breakthrough article in an obscure Polish medical journal, and convened the first world conference of ALD experts.

They devised a treatment they called "Lorenzo's Oil," and scoured the world until they found a company to produce the substance. It's not a cure, but it does stop production of the harmful fatty acids. Within weeks of being treated with it, Lorenzo's fatty acid levels dropped to normal. This was the first time in medical history that anyone had succeeded in normalizing VLCFA levels in an ALD patient.

"The oil is a mixture of grapeseed and olive oils that have been purified in a very sophisticated way," explains Michaela. "It inhibits the body's production of fatty acids. We use it in cooking Lorenzo's food."

Hundreds of ALD boys around the world are now taking

Lorenzo's Oil daily. Although the lengthy formal studies will not be completed until 1994, there is increasing evidence that boys who inherited the ALD gene but were presymptomatic before taking the oil have not developed symptoms. In children with symptoms as severe as Lorenzo's, the results are mixed.

"The oil is not a cure," explains Michaela. "But it prevents symptoms from developing, and in two cases we know of, symptoms have been reversed. The actual cure will come from therapy, which is still a ways off."

Fifteen-year-old Lorenzo Michael Murphy Odone has long since beaten his original two-year diagnosis. But unfortunately, in the three critical years it took for the Odones to develop Lorenzo's Oil, the disease did much damage to his body. He is a quadriplegic and cannot talk. But his mind is sharp and he "talks" with hand and eye gestures. His condition has improved within the last five years—he has regained continence, can sit in a wheelchair, move certain parts of his body when asked, and vocalize sounds that are music to his mother's years. He can see well enough to recognize people and can hear well enough to enjoy classical music. Amazingly, he still understands both French and English as well as some Italian. He's learning how to communicate with a computer.

"He's not just surviving," his mother says proudly. "He's living. Since the movie came out, some naysayers claim a few children have survived without the oil. But they don't mention the fact that these children are in a persistent vegetative stage and that Lorenzo is not.

"What we've done debunks the myth that you need to be an expert to make a difference. Ordinary people can make a difference. We need to believe that.

"As parents we must be brave for our children because God has given them to us. As their stewards, we should be dauntless."

Although the oil has halted the progress of ALD in Lorenzo's body, his myelin cannot repair itself. Further improvements are unlikely unless a way is found to help Lorenzo's myelin regenerate itself. So it is toward this ambitious goal that his parents are now devoting their extraordinary energies.

Once again they are refusing to relinquish their child to fate. Again they are changing the reality of their lives through commitment, positive action and faith. Driven by their determination to see Lorenzo walking, talking and laughing again, the Odones launched the Myelin Project in 1989. Headed by Augusto, this privately funded effort is totally dedicated to researching remyelination and stimulating cooperation among research groups around the world.

Dramatic new cell-transplant therapies are being tested to induce the central nervous system to regenerate its missing myelin; repair damaged nerves; and restore motion, sensation and vision. Initial experiments show promise. Since the movie, thousands of sponsors offering support and scores of ALD families desperate for information have called the Odones' toll-free number, 1-800-8-MYELIN. If this project succeeds, it will benefit not only ALD sufferers but all victims of demyelinating diseases, such as multiple sclerosis.

"It's a race against the clock," says Michaela. "Every minute counts in this battle. Lorenzo and a multitude of others are depending on us."

With Power Thinking, a fierce love for the son

entrusted to them, and God's help, the Odones have already accomplished the impossible. God willing, they'll do it again.

What if the Odones had surrendered to the fear of failure? What if they had not attempted the impossible?

Power Thinkers handle their Power Thoughts with courage! Then . . .

6

"IT IS IMPOSSIBLE TO FAIL COMPLETELY AND IT'S IMPOSSIBLE TO SUCCEED PERFECTLY."

Power Thinkers are not afraid of failure. If fear of failure is a problem for you—

Try this Power Thought. PICK YOUR FAILURES CAREFULLY. I have. I chose to fail in golf—so I could succeed in writing books, and building a Crystal Cathedral. I chose to fail with some negative thinking Christians—so I could succeed in building friendships and help some wonderful unbeliever find the faith.

Just use these Power Thoughts. It's impossible to fail completely if you will dare to try.

But if you try and fail won't this label you a total failure? No way!

You succeeded first in the role of a leader. You were decisive.

You showed the courage to make a commitment.

You were a winner on the levels where courage is honored.

You dared to try.

You succeeded as a researcher.

You successfully demonstrated one way that can be set aside and not replicated.

The person who attempts to do something great and fails cannot possibly be a <u>total</u> failure.

But consider the person who is so "ego-involved" that his pride will not let him attempt to do something great because he fears that if he fails, he will be embarrassed and humiliated, and suffer an ego blowout!

This person runs the real risk of being a total failure.

Great people who dare to face the risk of failure succeed in the business of great character development. They have demonstrated integrity. The heart of a truly great person has integrity at its core.

You must be an honest steward of your gift.

<u>YOUR</u> DREAM IS GOD'S GIFT TO YOU.

You must be faithful to that treasured trust that God has deposited in your life. Succeed or fail, you must be faithful first—and that means humbling yourself enough to dare to try!

Real humility is knowingly exposing yourself to a commitment to attempt something that you know may turn out to be a failure. That's the positive fulfillment of the charge Jesus gave to his disciples. "If any man would be my follower, let him deny himself, take up his cross and follow me."

•   •   •

Of all the guests I've had in over a thousand telecasts, the person that is remembered most of all is John Croyle. I checked him out—after I heard this remarkable story:

The freight train stopped before sunrise in a lonely little town. A few men walked up to one car, slid the doors open, looked into the darkness inside with flashlights, preparing to put something in there; what they saw hovering, shivering, trembling, in the corner was a little boy holding onto an empty cereal box. They were shocked. "What'll we do with him?" someone asked. Immediately one of the the men said, "Oh, that's an easy decision. We'll just send him to John Croyle."

John Croyle was an outstanding football player in college. He played for my friend Coach Bear Bryant at the University of Alabama. He was one of their greatest stars, playing in three bowl games.

I called and invited him to be a guest on my TV program.

This tall, lanky, handsome young man with the quick smile and southern drawl shook my hand with a strong grasp. I liked him immediately! I said, "We had a mutual friend. He was your coach, Bear Bryant."

"Yes, sir. He was tough. You know, someone asked, 'How tough was he?' and I said, 'How tough did you hear? It was worse than that.'"

"While you played on that team, under Coach Bryant, you went to the bowl three times, right?"

"Yes, sir, sure did. We only lost one regular season game in three years. And so, you know, <u>winning was under-</u>

stood. It was not something we had a choice in. You had to win or you walked home. And that's tough, you know, when you're in Texas or L.A. That's Lower Alabama, not Los Angeles or anything like that." His laugh filled the room.

"But John, even though you were offered lucrative professional football career opportunities after you graduated, you had this Power Thought, 'I'd like to help troubled kids.' So instead of playing pro ball, you decided to follow the Power Thought and start a boys' home."

"Yes, sir. I just can't stand to see somebody hurt a child.

"I was in McDonald's and this guy pulled his boy by the ear and was hurting him, and I said, 'Mister, you want to see how that feels?'" Laughing, John added, "It's amazing how quickly he let go of the little boy's ear.

"That's my gift. I can't preach like you can, but give me a little boy or a little girl that's hurting. Over the years I've put together the staff and raised the money to create children's homes in Arkansas, Georgia, two in Tennessee, and one in Colorado. It started with one, but there were too many hurting kids for one home. We just had to start more."

Power Thoughts have the power to multiply! Great dreams of great dreamers are never fulfilled, they're always transcended.

"What are you doing for girls?" I asked him.

"Well, I was only nineteen years old when I met a little boy from the streets of New Orleans. His mother was a prostitute. He was his mother's cash collector and timekeeper. I told the little boy how he could become a Christian. And he became a Christian and Jesus Christ changed his life. That's when I knew we needed a home for boys.

"Then several years later, I met a little girl who was twelve years old. She had been raped by her father while her mother held her down. I tried to adopt the little girl, but they wouldn't let me have her. They sent the girl back home and the father killed her. I made a promise to God that when the time was right we'd build a home for girls. And we worked a long time on it.

"Now, three years later, we have 325 acres completely paid for. We have three children's homes, we have twenty-two girls living on a girls' ranch. The girls' houses are identical to the boys' houses except the girls have got more plumbing needs than we guys have got, so, you know, we had to change all the plumbing in the house for the girls. The neat thing about this is let's say we find a family of five brothers and sisters, we can take the boys and put them in one place and put the girls in another place. And that's how we've been able to help families, you know, stay together."

"How would you say some of these kids are, what would you say, 'naughty kids'?"

"Naughty? Is that what you all say out here? Naughty?"

"What do you say in Alabama?"

"They're bad kids . . . no, they're not bad kids. It's just they've been taught some things that weren't correct. And, what we try to do is, we say, 'Now look, you've been told your whole life that you can't do this, and you can't do that, and you're bad, you're a no-account, you're a sorry person. That's not true. God don't make no junk and He don't make garbage and you are not a mistake. And no matter what your parents say to you, you're mine now and we're going to fly now. Get ready to fly.'"

"You gave them positive—life-changing—new Power Thoughts!"

I continued. "You're married and have a family, right? How do their little minds react to all of this?"

"Well, sir, I've got two children, aged thirteen and nine. You know, we've had over 1,200 kids since we started . . . How do my kids handle it? Well, the best example I can give you is that children watch your example.

"One day a man drove in my driveway and he had three little boys in the back of his car. And he said, 'I want you to take my three boys.'

"And I said, 'Okay, you go talk to a staff member and I'll go talk to the boys.'

"I took the boys into my home and said, 'Boys, your dad's got some problems, and he's really having a hard time. You all are going to stay with us for a while.' The older boy looked at me and said, 'No more war? No more getting beat up? No more going hungry? Sounds like a good deal to me!' And he got up and started playing one of the video games. The younger brother grabbed the side of his head and pulled his head down between his knees and he started screaming, 'I told you he was going to dump us, but you didn't listen to me.'

"So I had a staff member carry him into another room. It took him six hours to get that little boy to quit screaming and crying. And then I looked at the little six-year-old brother. The hardest thing I've ever had to do was reach around that daddy's neck and pull that little boy's fingers apart. And all the time he had his face buried in his daddy's cheeks, saying, 'You're my daddy. You can't leave me here.'

"Then I carried him into the bathroom. I said, 'Buddy, we got to have a bath before we eat 'cause you stink.'

"I took his shoes off. He had quarter-sized holes on the back of his ankles where the skin was gone 'cause the shoes were so small. And when I pulled his shirt up he had burns and cuts on his stomach, side and back, where he'd been abused.

"I picked him up and turned around after I'd given him a bath, and saw my own little five-year-old son standing in the doorway. In his arms were all of his clothes and pajamas and underwear. He said to the naked, bruised, broken boy in my arms, 'Here, you ain't got any clothes. You can have mine.'

"After he was dressed, my nine-year-old daughter said, 'Come here, we need to fix your cuts.' And she put Band-Aids and Neosporin on his cuts. I'll tell you, Dr. Schuller, if I can teach my children to love like that, then I'll die a successful man."

•   •   •

Yes, try to do a beautiful impossibility—and you'll never be a total failure. You'll build real character on the heroic level.

And then what? How can you be inoculated against the potentially devastating thing called perfectionism? By simply knowing <u>nobody is perfect</u>. No performance is beyond flaw in every facet. No pitcher ever won a game in baseball by throwing only eighty-one straight strikes in nine innings.

And when and where we don't succeed perfectly we learn something.

A boy asked his father as they painted their corn barn, "When did you build this barn?"

156

"Thirty-two years ago," the smiling dad replied.

"You sure know how to build good foundations, Dad."

Father smiled again. "Yep. You know why this one is so good? 'Cause the first one failed."

—— 7 ——
"THE FUTURE HAS MANY ALTERNATIVES."

Power Thinkers empower their thinking with creative energy which rejects cynicism and dispels pessimism.

Negative thinking experts paint bleak and bitter pictures of the future. With unchallengeable "authority," they will extrapolate the end results of trends and "prove" what disasters are going to befall the human race. Almost without exception, in time, the negative conclusions are proven to have been exaggerated as first reported.

Power Thinkers do not deny the horrific realities of the danger tracks that run dangerously loose in society, but neither do they underestimate the unpredictable positive reactions of a single person to release a power thought that will change everything! They believe that:

> "THE FUTURE WILL CHOOSE WHERE IT
> SHOULD GO—AND WHAT IT SHOULD BE."

And Power Thinkers make friends with the future and help shape it successfully:

This POWER THOUGHT will empower optimism which is the mental climate of dynamic creativity.

One of my closest friends was Dr. Armand Hammer. I

credit him with being the catalyst that cracked the will of Communism. He was a friend of Lenin and worked closely with every leader in Russia except for Stalin. "I couldn't deal with him. He was a really bad man," Hammer said.

"Dr. Schuller, you've got to come to my office." It was Dr. Hammer. He had just returned from Moscow for the funeral of Chernenko and the installation of his successor, Mikhail Gorbachev. Now six days later I was alone with Dr. Hammer in his Los Angeles office. I never saw him as excited as he was then and there. "Dr. Schuller, I had to tell you to come. We must pray. I truly believe we are going to see Russia change. I've got to tell you what happened! I was in the front of the line in the reception for the new man Gorbachev. He invited me into his private quarters. We spent an hour and a half together. I felt a tremendous motivation to be completely frank with him.

"'Mr. Gorbachev, I'm so happy to meet you,' I said, continuing, 'I have known every leader of this country starting with Lenin.

"'Now, first just let me say that you are the first educated leader since Lenin that this Communist country has had.

"'Second, you are the first young man to take the top job. All of the others were old men.

"'Third, you have a smart wife. She is well-educated and intelligent.

"'Next, you have the freedom and the jet planes to travel all over the world and visit any free country and see how capitalism as a free market economy works.

"'Compare your system with ours. You'll see. You'll know. Your system will never make it. Mr. Gorbachev, my father was a founding member of the Communist Party in America. He pleaded with me to reject capitalism and become a leader in Communism and socialism. I argued with my dad and finally said, "Dad, I can't and I won't—for it will never work! It goes against human nature." Mr. Gorbachev, you are the man who could see this! Admit to this! Lead your people to freedom.' "

Hammer's hope hammered this aggressive challenge home to Gorbachev: "Become the Abraham Lincoln of Russia." The result: Gorbachev listened. He was a good audience. He wrote a classic book, *Perestroika*. Years later, I was photographed with Dr. Hammer as the two of us left Los Angeles for Moscow in Hammer's private plane.

En route to Russia, Dr. Hammer said, "Now Dr. Schuller, we'll ask Gorbachev to open the doors in his country to religion. I'll ask him to let you preach a sermon about 'The God of Love.' "

A meeting was held the next day. It was a three-hour meeting. "Well, Dr. Schuller," the Minister of Television said to me with Hammer listening. "We have been and still are atheists, but we have come to believe that there are some positive factors that only seem to come into humans through religion.

"So, Dr. Schuller," he continued, "we now invite you to be the first foreign preacher to be invited to go on our atheist television Channel 1 and preach a twenty-minute sermon. You will make history. You will go into a studio today. We will record it. It will be aired on Sunday night, December 25, 1989! It will be listened to by over 200 million Russians. For this has never ever happened before in our nation! And you

are our enemy. You are an American. The Cold War is still on. Do a good job and maybe we will no longer be afraid of religion—or afraid of Americans."

Everything he promised—happened!

Five months later I was invited to preach again, a sermon to be aired the night before Gorbachev would leave for the May 1990 Summit in Washington. Gorbachev was so impressed he invited me to lunch with him that week at the Russian embassy in Washington. This led to invitations for me to become the first minister of any religion to broadcast a message every Sunday morning on Channel 1 to his entire country.

On Thursday, April 29, 1993, I would have a warm visit with Gorbachev in Moscow. He presented me with one of my most treasured gifts: an autographed copy of *Perestroika,* with a full-page, handwritten message from Gorbachev to Schuller.

The next day I was called to the office of Boris Yeltsin's chief of staff. It was Friday, April 30, 1993.

"Dr. Schuller," the chief of staff said, "last Sunday, April 25, Yeltsin's reform movement was saved! He won the election. If he had lost, the Parliament of old Communists would have taken over.

"It was the most crucial time in our young history. Sunday morning I locked my door, turned that television on here in the heart of the Kremlin and from 8 to 9 a.m., you were on and were with me here. When you were finished, I said, 'That message of Dr. Schuller's will win the day for Yeltsin.'

"Dr. Schuller, over 10 million people here have lis-

160

tened to you every Sunday for over one year now—fifty-six Sundays. You have taught them what they have never been told before. You teach them to 'Believe in yourself.' You teach them that we are human beings, created by God. We have brains. We can think. We can trust our thoughts. Dr. Schuller, you teach this every week. 'Believe in the God who made you and believe in yourself.' Communism never, never, never wanted that teaching to get out! They don't want us to think for ourselves. They want us to listen to them and obey. They didn't educate us, they indoctrinated us!"

Yes, the future is open to the most unbelievable options! I never thought I'd live to see Communism defeated and freedom take over in Russia. This would surely be the most exciting, discretionary move I'd see history make!

God only knows the power of a single Power Thought!

Yes—the future has many alternatives.

World—watch out! The future will be shaped by the person who believes in himself or herself.

Now, Power Thinkers—get ready to change the world!

I think we can! On the next page is a letter I received from Gorbachev.

The International Foundation for Socio-Economic Studies
(The Gorbachev Foundation)
49, Leningrad Prospekt
Moscow 125468

Dear Dr. Schuller,

I received your letter in which you warmly recall our recent meeting in Moscow. I also have the best memory of that meeting.

I think your proposal is promising to promote our friendly relations between the peoples of our countries. A cause that was so fitting to Armand Hammer's initiative and to which he gave so much of his creative efforts. In the name of these noble goals that guide me, the International Foundation is open to diverse communication with you. For one, we would probably be interested also in the project sponsored by the Crystal Cathedral Office in Moscow to assist Russian farmers, which you mentioned in your letter.

My staff, Dr. Schuller, welcomes direct contact with your Moscow office on any specific issue of possible cooperation.

Best wishes,
Mikhail Gorbachev
July 21, 1993

Yes—let's change our world for the next century!

6

Power Thinkers,
Let's Just
Change Our World!

The twentieth century!—1900 to 1999!

It's almost over.

What will the twentieth century be remembered for? Many things we shall recall. Probably most of all, this may be called the Century of the Collectivist.

The twenty-first century? What does it hold? God only knows. But I hope and pray it will be the Century of the Redeemed Individualist.

Yes, this astounding century—this twentieth century-- is rapidly ending.

In the <u>fifteenth century</u> came the discovery that the world is round!

The sixteenth century brought global exploration. Continents were discovered—floating on oceans on the other side of this spinning round ball called "earth."

The seventeenth century saw the establishment of European colonies around the world.

The eighteenth century was marked by one hundred years of a transatlantic business called human slavery.

Human slavery had always been a social plague. Victorious armies took captured enemies home as slaves—cheap labor. But never before 1619 was there a global industry where African tribes were plundered of their men and women and had them harvested, held and sold on open markets. Twenty million were manacled, marched and marketed for nearly 250 years.

The nineteenth century:

• The expansion and entrenchment of imperialism, colonialism.

• The rise of industrialization.

• The oppressive power of capitalism, often without a conscience.

• Exploitation of human talent and energy and skill, below ground in mines, and above ground in factories and sweat shops.

• Economic injustice exploited and victimized children in child labor; women as well as men; whites as well as all other colors.

The twentieth century:

The twentieth century—1900 to 1999. No one in 1900 could come close to predicting what the twentieth century would see unfolding.

Bad things! World War I, World War II, the Holocaust. The Cold War. Thermonuclear weapons. AIDS.

Good things, too! Telephones. Electricity. Radio. Television. Jet airplanes. Computers. Cheerios. Instant satellite communications.

Humans walking on the moon.

A vaccine against polio.

Transplantation of body organs.

Contact lenses.

Antibiotics.

BUT NOW THE REALLY BAD NEWS:

By 1900,

the hurting, humiliated, hopeless, helpless, hungry family of human beings

were ripe and ready for

what would be a devastating, reactionary revolution!

Enter the teachings of Karl Marx.

Communism was conceived.

Collectivism became a movement to challenge and condemn inhumane individualism, and insulting individualism.

Socialism versus capitalism would meet to be the chief combatants on the economic battlefields for seventy years in this twentieth century.

Socialism, Communism and collectivism offered hope-filled help to relieve suffering victims of social, racial, political, economic, and religious oppression and injustice.

Economists joined the movement. So did psychologists. Freud was considered an enemy of Marx. For Freudianism focused on the individual.

Religious leaders in Christianity—both Catholic and Protestant—listened and related Marxist principles to their teachings. Even some leaders in Islam and Judaism picked up on Marxism.

Collectivism became a new paradigm inspiring revolutionary interpretations of the Bible.

Prominent liberal theologians would attack the religious writers, thinkers and preachers whose ministry and message were aimed at helping the individual versus "restructuring society."

The strong appeal to individualism was seen as a threat to collectivism. So in the 1950s, Norman Vincent Peale with his "power of positive thinking" became the target for attack. Collectivist Christians would label this positive-thinking Christian movement as "mercenary; materialistic; selfish and self-centered." Preachers who talked to the single, solitary soul with its private sins and hurts, dreams and hopes, were accused of practicing "religious expressions devoid of a redeeming social conscience."

Socialistic economics would have a deep and wide impact on the theological thinking of Protestantism and Catholicism.

I entered my professional life smack in the middle of this twentieth century. I was ordained in 1950. I stepped right in the middle of this steaming, searing, philosophical battle, between the colliding paradigms—collectivism and individualism! I was innocently and naïvely unaware of the existence of the conflict.

The first forty years of my ministry would be operated

under this cloud of philosophical conflict. I would be praised and condemned, sought and ignored, not knowing why.

I would believe, preach, and practice what I called "Possibility Thinking." Its appeal, I now understand, was unintentionally, but intuitively aimed at the individualist. I was really teaching and preaching what I now call "Redemptive Individualism." It would be warmly welcomed in Moscow in 1992!

REDEMPTIVE INDIVIDUALISM

What is Redemptive Individualism? It's a message aimed at the private person—not the "religious club."

"Salvation is individualistic—not Socialistic."

"You are redeemed individually by Christ—not collectively by a member of the correct church."

"Success is individualistic—not socialistic."
You have to set your goals!
You have to make your personal decisions.
You have to make your dreams come true.
Society won't give you what you want.
You have to make it happen!

Power Thinking—yes, it's a friendly, and fair, and frank appeal to the private person who was born alone, will die alone, and will succeed or fail alone.

Others must help. But, you—and only you alone—can build your dream. And you and only you can make it live or let it die.

Redemptive Individualism. This means that when you

succeed, you will help redeem those who need help.

"Saved to serve," old preachers used to say.

"Redemptive Individualism."

God wants to turn persons into caring creatures.

God wants to honor humans by using us to redeem lost souls.

A decent, thoughtful priest was walking home late one night and saw a pathetic drunk lying in the gutter. Suddenly, he found himself under a horrific attack from a cynical thought and he prayed, "Oh, God, if you are really alive, why do you let this man lie in shame? If you truly exist, why don't you help him?"

And into this man of God's mind came this sentence: "I am helping him. I just brought him to your attention."

This Gospel would be praised and applauded by some and cynically criticized by others. It would be called an "American" religious expression of Christianity by the collectivists. Oddly, it would be warmly welcomed first in Korea! "Dr. Schuller, your flagship book, *Move Ahead with Possibility Thinking,* saved my ministry in its dark and young days," Paul—later to be named David—Yonggi Cho would say. His church would grow into the largest Christian church in the world by the 1990s and would reach one million members. In 1992 one of its elders would be elected as the first truly democratic and nonmilitary president of South Korea.

I would spend my life torn between so-called Christian Communists, Christian anti-Communists and Christian anti-anti-Communists.

Later, I would find myself strangely called and positioned to bring the first public television sermons to all of

Russia, coming from the heart of Orange County, California, U.S.A.

I could find myself speaking, teaching, preaching to more persons in Russia and the world every week than any other religious spokesman in their history. As I write these lines, that is still the scene today.

I've been a point man—ahead of the front line—to witness the dissolution of old boundaries.

The death of Communism, the discrediting of socialism and the disillusionment with collectivism have occurred.

A deep cynicism has resulted.

"The government has let us down" is the pathetic lament of the peasants under Communism.

"The government has let us down" is the cynical complaint of whites and blacks in South Africa.

"The government has let us down" is the angry cry from more than one segment of hurting American society as this twentieth century—this "collectivist" century—now comes to an end. We're ready for Power Thinkers who are redemptive individuals.

Welcome, Century 21

Now take a trip with me and catch a vision of the next century, 2000–2099!

This could very possibly be the greatest century in which humans have ever lived since we have existed on the planet earth. What's in store for humans, and all the other creatures on planet earth from the year 2000 'til the year 2099?

POWER THINKERS, LISTEN!

Burt Rutan, builder of the *Voyager,* is one of the really great Power Thinkers on the scientific cutting edge. I've asked him to be my guest on my television program. What I heard him say was really twenty-first-century power thinking.

"We are living today for the first time in history when we can kill a lake. But also for the first time in history we can clean a lake.

"For the first time in history we have detected ozone loss—but for the first time in history, we can replace that lost ozone.

"We will <u>be</u> <u>able</u> <u>to</u> solve problems we <u>never</u>, <u>ever</u> imagined were solvable. But will we do so?"

We will be able to clean the air, clean the rivers and the streams, purify drinking waters out of the salty seas, turn the deserts into fresh, healthy farmlands, and feed billions more human beings than we ever expected could live healthy, happy lives on this planet.

The next century? It will be fabulous beyond all predictions—if leadership is claimed and captured by Positive Thinkers, Possibility Thinkers, Power Thinkers! That's you! That's me. That's our children, and our grandchildren and our great-grandchildren.

Humans who have their "internal thought processors" connected will see the screens of their imaginations light up with the vision that comes from the cosmic, creative command center. Messages will be received in our systems. Messages from God to humans!

Let's join with God and power will be turned on. God wanted the globe to be a gorgeous garden for humans to live,

170

and love and feel his presence in the whisper of the wind, in the shafts of light out of the darkness. In the reflections of water drops on a leaf!

Which is why many Power Thinkers are also incurably attracted and addicted to beauty. There's power in the heart of beauty. God planned it that way.

I was still conducting services every Sunday in a drive-in theater when I hired the world-famed architect Richard Neutra to design my first church. His profound influence on my life is beyond calculation. Richard Neutra picked up the seminal ideas of René Dubos and produced an architectural philosophy called "Bio-Realism." I learned it from him.

The architect drew plans of a beautiful church. We set out to design a church that would be dominated by "sky and gardens." For years, that great architect lectured to me. He profoundly created in my consciousness an overwhelming environmental awareness.

"The human was designed and engineered to be a 'spiritual creature,'" Neutra said, "to receive and send spiritual signals, and messages from the Creator Himself. So our eyes and ears and nose and skin were intended to be sources to pick up sensations that would tranquilize the creature called man. And this deep relaxation would put him in quiet moods where he could 'think,' 'feel,' 'hear'—CREATE. In his natural habitat—God's Garden—he would naturally be a positive, spiritual Power Thought Processor."

I delivered that lecture to over 4,000 architects from around the world in the opening address of the American Architectural Convention in St. Louis. I was, at the time, a member of the board of directors of the American Institute of Architects.

"How many of you were taught 'Bio-Realism' when you were in the university?" I asked.

Relatively few hands went up.

"Let me teach you," I offered. And in a forty-minute lecture I shared what I learned under my years of private tutoring by Richard Neutra, with the ideas of René Dubos mixed in. I was never more proud to receive a standing ovation than when I received one from that audience that morning.

René Dubos discovered that biological organisms had a sociological behavior. It was his observation and his contribution to twentieth-century knowledge that "Every biological organism lives in its own sociological environment. Change that environment and you kill the organism. But before the organism will be killed," he said, "it will become a deviant, adjusting to survive.

"And," Dubos said, "it always adjusts downward in its struggle to survive." I said to him, "Adjustment is always a downward movement. The upper movement never comes through adjustment, it's always a <u>commitment</u>." And we all agreed on that. Dubos, the sociobiologist, talking with the great architect Richard Neutra, inspired him to create a doctrine of biological realism.

What's that?

It means that the human being was designed to live in a garden. That's our natural habitat. And if we are moved out of the garden we will adjust downward in order to survive. Put us in a place where there is concrete, asphalt, power poles, sirens, squealing brakes, sounds of yelling and gunfire,

172

and we will lose our profound deep inner tranquillity and peace. At that point we will not hear the "still small voice of God." And we will become deviant. The result? Doubters instead of believers. Doubt is an abnormality. Faith is a normality. Remember? We just said that.

So when we created the world's first walk-in drive-in church on ten acres, the architect planned for a long row of cypress trees, which would rise tall and green and tranquil along the main entrance to the church. The church board took a look at that and cut it out.

"It'll cost too much money to water the trees, to prune the trees, and we'd like a wider driveway," they said. So they ruled out the trees and planned all asphalt. It was a horrible mistake.

I corrected the situation. I hired a bulldozer to rip out the asphalt. I had a load of thirty beautiful little cypress trees delivered to be planted. They were planted. They stand today. Beauty! I am addicted to it!

The twenty-first century? I envision world leadership in the careful, dareful, prayerful hands of Power Thinkers addicted to beauty. In architecture, in landscaping. In personality. In language. In music. In emotional construction. In the collection and care of our memories. Beauty drives me.

Jesus taught it. "Man shall not live by bread alone." Absolutely not. The heart has its own hunger. In the fragrance of a flower, the song of a bird. The shaping of a cloud, the drifting of a wave across white sand, all of this is beauty that can tranquilize, and remove stress, and put creative energy deep in the heart.

"Beauty Is Practical, Too" was the title of one of

Richard Neutra's profound essays in a book on architecture. "If you think it's practical just to pave it—remember this," he said. "Green grass, blooming flowers, sweeping trees and beautiful pools of quiet water are beautiful and are very, very, very practical for human beings also!"

Power Thinkers—in the twenty-first century let's turn the globe into a garden again.

We can. We will. And humanity will move from cold, cynical, skeptical, distrusting, tense, stress-filled, violence-inclined creatures to tranquil, creative souls.

Let's plan a beautiful world for the next hundred years!

We can change our world.

We will change the next century!

Using these Power Thoughts:

POWER THOUGHT
#1

"I'm committed to succeed as a Power Thinker."

How will Power Thinkers respond and react to the problems and possibilities that are already here?

I prayed to God on what I should write in this space. I turned my Spiritual Thought Processor on and waited. I probed and pressed the spiritual buttons of my internalized computer. A message appeared out of my memory systems, triggered by the Holy Spirit of God.

"Tell your readers what I told you to tell Possibility

Thinkers twenty years ago—'How to react to glorious, impossible ideas.'"

"Thank You, Lord."

I remember! Here it is:

Handle Power Thoughts darefully,

carefully, prayerfully.

1. Be a <u>WOW</u> Thinker. Listen: Does the idea shock
       you superpositively? It probably
       came from God. Listen to it.

2. Be a NOW Thinker. Do something with it now.
       Today. Write it down in your journal.
       Telephone another Super Power Thinker.
       Don't let it fall in those black holes that
       are right around you.

3. Be a HOW Thinker. Keep asking "How." Answers
       will come, names will be called to your
       attention. Perhaps competitors. Old
       antagonists? Think of this Power
       Thought: Move from a mental attitude
       of collision to coalition. Stop fighting
       and start cooperating. What could you
       do if you turned your competitor into
       your partner?

4. Be a VOW Thinker. Make a decision never to let
       the dream die. Hold it in your heart as
       long as you live. Keep lines open with
       God and someday—

5. POW!—the rocket will be launched! The impossible will happen! Hello, hero!

POWER THOUGHT
#2

"If it's going to be, it's up to me."

General Dwight Eisenhower often used these three Power Thought words: "<u>enlightened self-interest</u>." No one will be more interested in you—than you. And that's very natural and appropriate.

So pray prayers that can make you into the person God wants you to be,

"How, Lord, can I become the best person possible?"

"How, Lord, can I become more helpful to more people?"

"How, Lord, can I become less of a burden to others and inspire others to do likewise?"

The next century will see more people with more problems than any government could possibly afford to help. You and I have to make help happen!

You and I must think with strength. "How can I be strong and successful enough to encourage, inspire and motivate others to rise from poverty to prosperity?"

The world doesn't give me a living—

"If it's going to be, it's up to me."

176

Society won't give you moral and ethical character—
"If it's going to be, it's up to me."

The university will not give you an education—
"If it's going to be, it's up to me."

Business doesn't owe me a job—
"If it's going to be, it's up to me."

Psychology cannot give me joy and happiness—
"If it's going to be, it's up to me."

Religious institutions will not save my soul—
"If it's going to be, it's up to me."

The minister who unites me in marriage to my spouse
won't give me a lifetime of happiness and harmony—
"If it's going to be, it's up to me."

The medical establishment can't give me good health—
"If it's going to be, it's up to me."

The national econonmy will not deliver financial security to my purse—
"If it's going to be, it's up to me."

A new sunrise doesn't promise to give me a great day—
"If it's going to be, it's up to me."

POWER THOUGHT
#3
*"We can and must learn how to help people
without doing more harm than good."*

We learned this when our thirteen-year-old daughter had a leg amputated. The greatest pain for us was not "helping" her every time she called and cried for help. She'd still be a cripple using close relationships as crutches. George Wannamaker was once asked, "What's the hardest job you've ever had to tackle?" His answer: "The hardest job for all of us is how to give away money without doing more harm than good." Communism never learned that lesson. Collectivism forgot the warning.

How do we help without doing more harm than good?

1. By inspiring persons to believe in themselves!

2. By offering help that encourages persons to <u>make it happen themselves</u>.

3. By keeping this noble end in mind all the time! And that's giving a person a chance to discover or recover his pride! His dignity! His self-respect! His self-esteem!

Dr. Floyd Baker, a member of my church, is a professor of physics. He wrote a special paper for his doctorate in physics. In it is an illuminating confession. Listen to him:

"When I first entered the teaching profession I brought with me a set of attitudes toward instruction and student-teacher interaction.

"Now in retrospect, I had what I know today to be a bad attitude toward my students and their motivation.

"I recall I used to say to them at the beginning of the semester, 'You have to pass this course or you might as well change your major.

"'I am the ONLY one teaching this class, so you might as well get along as best you can.

"'I don't like people who won't study, so get on the ball!

"'I give you material and all you have to do is learn it. Let me tell you, about fifty percent of you won't pass. Don't let it be YOU!'

"Well, amazingly, my predictions always came true. Fifty percent flunked out—always, year after year.

"I would get together with the other college professors and we would drink coffee and we would laugh at the number of dropouts that we had in our classes. We used to say that the one who had the most dropouts was the most successful teacher.

"I know now that this is a bad attitude.

"About this time, my wife and I started attending a very dynamic church. The ministers were all enthusiastic and all preached outstanding sermons.

"Each week when I attended church I was deluged with the need for positive thinking and enthusiasm in everything you do. I discovered that you are always received better if you have a positive attitude when visiting or talking to people. However, my problem was, How could I inspire and enthuse my students?

"The ministers kept saying, 'If you have a problem, through prayer and reading the Bible, you can find the answer.' I started reading my Bible, chapter after chapter, book after book. I came to First Corinthians 13 and I found the key. From then on, Christ was in my life. I went in front of my class and I said to them,

" 'I want every one of you to pass. And it is my job to see that you do. The material is difficult, but if we work together, every student in this class can pass and learn a great deal.'

"There was a different atmosphere in the classes from then on and I thank God and Christ for this spirit. The dropout and failure rate prior to Christ being in my classroom was fifty percent. However, when I applied this new positive technique, with the cooperation of the students, every student passed! One received a C-plus, one a B-minus, and the rest all got B's and A's and I NEVER CHANGED MY GRADING PROCEDURE ONE BIT!"

POWER THOUGHT
#4
"No person can succeed without helping people."

Is there a simple secret for success? Will it work for me? Can I share it with others? Can it be a positive prescription to lift persons from poverty—to Pride of Achievement?

What's poverty? You are not in poverty if you can afford to be a philanthropist and give money away to help others. That's why I never felt poor. I went to church every Sunday of my life and as a little child, my father put a coin in my hand to drop in the offering plate. The older I got and get, the more I'm able to increase my giving. By contrast, I know people who have net worths of millions of dollars and in their mental framework, they never are "able to give."

Years ago, I penned a message to motivate myself to keep on keeping on! I remember and still use the talk built around:

S.T.R.I.V.E.

Start <u>small</u>. I did. Two members, and $500. We started a church. We started small in television: one station twenty-four years ago. Today we're on nearly two hundred stations.

Think <u>tall</u>. I did. We dreamed of moving from one TV station to three. Three years later, we expanded to six. Our secret dream was to cover the entire U.S.A. I know how to succeed, but I don't know how to do it in a hurry.

Reach over the <u>wall</u>. When obstacles block you, look beyond them. Think longer, think bigger. When you can't see through the wall, look over and beyond it.

Invest <u>your all.</u> Really. Most people fail not because of problems, obstacles or competition; they fail because they don't give their dream all they've got!

Visualize <u>the ball</u>! Dream about the party you'll have. Imagine ultimate success: Hold mental pictures of the tenth anniversary party.

Expect to <u>stall</u>. Maybe stumble, maybe get stuck. Expect this! And you'll wait it out. Work it out and <u>never fall.</u>

Now succeed!

Leave no room for final failure. Your success can help so many people in your world who need hope.

POWER THOUGHT
#5
"I am being born again as a redeemed Individualist by God to change the world."

Once more: What's a "redemptive individual"? Well, it's a solitary soul who's been redeemed from the sins that allow him to run roughshod over anybody who stands in his way toward selfish success. This rugged individual is redeemed—changed! Born again!—to a life of really caring about people. Redemptive individualism is Christianity at its best.

This new century about to be born calls for new Christian Power Thinkers to lift and liberate persons—

from war to peace,

from oppression to liberation,

from poverty to prosperity,

from alienation to community,

from collision to coalition,

from selfishness to sacrificial service with a sweet spirit,

from serfdom to self-reliance, self-respect, self-worth, self-confidence. "I can do all things through Christ who strengthens me." (Philippians 4:13)

Never before in human history has there been a more urgent need for the face and voice of positive faith to be seen and heard pouring from the healthy hearts of emotionally beautiful persons whose lives are controlled by their dynamic and beautiful faith in God and in Jesus Christ.

•   •   •

Yes, I invite you to come and live with me in another country called "Redemptive Individualism."

It is the "power place to be" in the world of the twenty-first century.

Come! Live where I have lived all of my life!

Accept my invitation to immigrate to this new world which offers real freedom! And hope! It's a <u>whole new world</u> for some of you.

"You can make it happen" is the slogan to inspire all of us who live here. It's the only world that offers the possibility to every person to dream of becoming a truly free person! Even financial independence is possible, permissible and encouraged in this world of Real Individualism!

<u>But first, a warning!</u> <u>Accept my invitation and this could kill you.</u> For there are potentially fatal spiritual and moral infections—certainly life-threatening infections—loose in this country of strong "individualism" where I ask you to live and breathe, dream and create, work and enjoy peace and prosperity. These dangerous and potentially catastrophic systemic infections are called Greed, Exploitation, Egotism, Selfishness, Oppression and Injustice.

But here's the good news. Immunity is possible! Vaccine is available! You can and you must get inoculated, getting your shots, and taking your special prescribed medication before you enter this fantastic new world called "Redemptive Individualism." Take the right prescription and you'll stand a great chance of becoming a successful, self-confident, generous, helpful, caring, kind, encouraging, really nice human being!

Now let me share with you how my relationship with Christ makes me a "Redemptive Individualist." I know him. I believe in him. I pray to him. He's my best friend.

THE REDEMPTIVE INDIVIDUAL'S PRAYER

Lord, I invite you to come and live your life in my life today.
Lord, here is my brain—think with it.
Lord, here is my face—smile through it.
Lord, here is my tongue—so speak to people with it.
Lord, here is my ear—listen to persons with it.
Lord, here is my hand—touch someone with it.
Lord, here are my arms—lift and hug someone with them.
Lord, here are my feet—walk with them where you want to go today.
Lord, I want to be a beautiful "Christ—In Person."

Amen

W.O.W. Wonder of Wonders!

I'm spiritually immunized to live, and work, and struggle, and play, and love—as I live in this world of Redemptive Individualism.

Century 21—Here we come!
Powerful people!
Beautiful people!
Power Thinkers!
"It is no longer we who live—but Christ who lives in us."

• • •

I have often led tours of people on world trips. Dozens of times the tours touched on several countries I had never seen before.

I'm planning my next tour and want to invite you to join me.

It's to a place I've never been before.

It's a place called "Tomorrow."

When we get there, they'll ask where we came from, and I'll say, "From yesterday."

Then they'll give each of us a gift! We'll accept it. Guess what it is? It's called "Today"!

HOW SWEET IT IS TO STAND ON THE
EDGE OF TOMORROW!

7

Power Thoughts
for
Power Living

Here's a special gift for you—today!
On the following pages are some "one page"
POWER THOUGHTS.
You'll be surprised to find "Just what you need
today!"

God loves you and so do I.

Robert Schuller

CURIOSITY LEADS TO CREATIVITY

Curiosity discovered America.
Curiosity put people on the moon.
Curiosity built Disneyland.
Be curious! Curiosity builds creativity.
Teachers know that their best students are driven by a desire to know and understand. Students want to find out about things that are hidden. They want to know what makes things work, how to do things for themselves.

Have you ever wondered about what you could accomplish if you told yourself anything is possible, instead of listening to people who tell you it's not possible?

Always be curious. What fascinates you? What improvements can you make? What can you invent that would make your life easier? How can you be a blessing to someone, somewhere today? Who would benefit from a contribution you can make?

Walt Disney said, "Curiosity is the key to making dreams come true." He always talked about being able to do amazing things because he refused to talk about the things he couldn't do. He accomplished great things because he didn't know he couldn't.

Curiosity is the brother of creativity. Remain curious and you will remain creative. Always believe you can do something bigger or better or more beautiful with your life, and you will.

GET GIANT POWER TO FACE YOUR GOLIATH

Remember the story of David and Goliath? David was a small shepherd boy who faced the greatest warrior of his time—Goliath. Goliath was a giant whose very presence struck fear into the entire Israeli army. No one would dare face Goliath, because they were sure they would be killed instantly.

They all said, "He's so big, we can't win."

David said, "He's so big, I can't miss."

That's self-confidence! David defeated Goliath. With a stone and a sling and something more—David had faith. David knew he could do it, because he believed that God was with him. David had a special faith.

With your special gift of faith you can believe that you can conquer and you will.

If there is a giant fear that looms like Goliath before you today and you say, "It's so big, I can't win," then know that God's power is greater than any fear you can imagine—even the fear of death. If you believe in God's power you can confront your Goliath with courage.

You'll be an "under-goer" who becomes an over-comer once you let God's power flow through you.

You Can Do It—Become A Conduit!

Can a pen change history? Yes, if it's in the hand of a president signing a contract.

Can a wire empower a factory building cars? Airplanes? Yes, if it connects a power source to a productivity center.

Can a tube be a lifesaver? Yes, if it connects an oxygen tank to a gasping lung.

Can a pipe feed the hungry and enrapture society with joyous beauty? Yes, if it is the conduit for water to irrigate the desert to produce food and grow flowers.

YOU CAN DO IT—if you will be a conduit.

Can I, a simple human, make a beautiful difference in this negative world?

Can a simple person like you or me really become the "life saver" where we are today? Yes—if we become the connection between God and some hurting, hoping, hungry, or haunted human you'll come close to today.

So you can do it ---if you'll be a conduit.

"Lord, lead me to the person you want to
speak to through my life today."
Amen.

189

BE PROUD OF WHO YOU ARE

I asked one of my colleagues, "What's one of the most vivid memories you have of going to school as a child?" Here's what he told me:

"In the third grade, we were asked to stand up in front of the class and say what we wanted to be when we grew up. Now, I went to a fairly strict school, and every time you were asked to stand before the class, it was a pretty serious matter.

"I remember very distinctly one girl who stood up and said, 'I'm going to be a movie star.'

"As I remember, there wasn't anything special about this girl. She wasn't very pretty. Her grades were average, some of them were even below average. She didn't come from a wealthy family. In fact, the only thing I really remember about her was the class laughing at her.

"The whole class laughed at her.

"And I remember she just stood there smiling, as if she knew something the rest of us didn't.

"I don't remember ever seeing that girl again in school. Now I see her all the time. She's one of the biggest stars in Hollywood. Every time I sit in the movie theater and watch her up there on the silver screen, I think, 'She was always so proud of who she was. She had a dream she always held onto.'

"Back then they laughed at her. Now they pay to see her. I'm glad I didn't laugh."

Be proud of who you are. You are someone who can make a difference in this world.

TREAT YOURSELF

Self-confidence comes from self-respect. You can do a lot to increase your self-confidence by improving the way you treat yourself.

When my youngest daughter Gretchen was in college, she lived at home to save money. I knocked on her door one afternoon.

"Come in," she said and I did.

I noticed there was a vase of fresh flowers on her desk. They were beautiful red roses.

"Who are these from?" I asked with a sly grin.

"Read the card," she said.

I picked a small, engraved card off the roses and opened it.

"Dear Gretchen," the card read, *"Many women do noble things, but you surpass them all. [Proverbs 31:29]*
                                                    Love, Jesus."

My eyes opened wide as I looked up at her.

"I sent them to myself," she said.

Treat yourself right. Take care of yourself and others will start treating you better. You deserve the best.

TRUST YOUR POSITIVE INSTINCTS

Keep yourself in tune with your God-inspired natural instincts, and you will keep yourself positive. Self-confidence will control your moods and actions, for God will be literally alive within! These positive impulses that stir within you are the powerful presence of God Himself living in you.

Norman Vincent Peale tells a story about Thomas Edison that I've always liked. This passage is from Peale's bestselling book *The Power of Positive Thinking*:

Mrs. Thomas Edison, with whom I often discussed the habits and characteristics of her famous husband, the world's greatest inventive wizard, told me that it was Mr. Edison's custom to come into the house from his laboratory after many hours of labor and lie down on his old couch. She said he would fall asleep as naturally as a child, in perfect relaxation, sinking into a deep and untroubled slumber. After three or four, or sometimes five hours he would become instantly wide awake, completely refreshed, and eager to return to his work.

"He was nature's man," Mrs. Edison said, by which she meant he was completely in harmony with nature and with God. In him there were no obsessions, no disorganizations, no conflicts, no mental quirks, no emotional instability. He worked until he needed to sleep, then he slept soundly and arose and returned to his work. He lived for many years, and was in many respects the most creative mind to appear on the American continent. He drew his energy from self-mastery. His amazing harmonious relationship with the universe caused nature to reveal to him its inscrutable secrets.

Thomas Edison was truly an amazing man. His genius changed communications, created the motion picture industry and made the world a better place for you and me.

Trust your positive instincts. Connect with the Power of Creativity that God has naturally designed within you.

YOU CAN BE IT—IF YOU CAN SEE IT

A beggar sat across the street from an artist's studio. From his window, the artist sketched the face of the poor, defeated soul. After the sketch was complete, the artist began to add color to the sketch of the beggar's face. As the brilliant hues of the oil paint brushed across the canvas, the beggar's face began to change.

Into the dull eyes the artist put the flashing glint of an inspired dreamer. He brightened the skin on the man's face to give him a look of iron will and fierce determination. He brushed the beggar's hair to give him a clean, regal look.

When the painting was finished, the artist called the poor beggar in to see it. The beggar did not recognize himself. "Who is it?" he asked quietly. The artist smiled.

The beggar looked at the painting closer, with a deeper appreciation. "Is it me?" he finally asked. *"Can* it be me?"

"Yes," replied the artist. "That's how I see you."

The beggar squared his shoulders, stood up tall and proudly said, "If that's the person you see—that's the person I'll be!"

God looks at you the way the artist does. He sees the person in you that you are meant to be. He sees the person He created you to be. Close your eyes and see the person you were meant to be. Hold this visual image of yourself. Look at the beautiful sparkle in your eyes. See how you hold your head up? See how your shoulders are squared and your back is straight? See how successful and self-confident you are? That's the person God wants you to be—a winner!

193

THE SECRET OF SELF-CONFIDENCE

I—I Am = I Can

C—Curiosity Builds Confidence

A—Anything Is Possible

N—Never Give Up

CHANGE—OR CHAINS! IT'S YOUR CHOICE

In my garden, I keep a small statue of a bronze elephant. It was a gift from friends in Bangkok, Thailand. The elephant stands about three feet tall and about four feet long. He is frozen in a position of total surrender. One of its legs is tied with an iron bracelet and chained to the small stem of a lotus flower that is stuck in the mud. This mighty elephant is chained to a flower stem, held captive because he believes he can't break the chains that bind him.

In Thailand, elephants from nearby jungles are captured and tamed. An iron band at the end of a heavy chain is secured around each elephant's foot and the elephant is chained to a large tree. The elephant lifts its leg and pulls, trying with all its might to break the chain or uproot the tree, but nothing ever happens. The elephant tries day after day, until it finally gives up. The powerful animal lifts its leg and feeling just a slight tension, places its foot back on the ground in complete submission. The elephant is trapped—loses its freedom—when it <u>thinks</u> it is still imprisoned.

The elephant is then taken out to work and tied to a small stake, sometimes only to the reed of a lotus flower. The elephant is trapped forever, even though with a slight effort he could easily break the chain and run free. <u>The elephant is trapped because he believes he can never break free.</u>

What chains do you <u>think</u> imprison you? What addiction keeps you trapped, when there is help and hope so available to give you freedom? You have the power to choose to break free today!

WHEN IT'S DARK, LOOK FOR THE STARS

Many people are afraid of the dark as kids. But I loved nighttime. I loved the pitch-blackness of Iowa nights because that was when the stars came out. I was fascinated by those tiny, twinkling lights. To me, every one of those stars was a possibility.

When you start to look for the stars, you're not afraid because you see all the possibilities that await you. Possibilities are opportunities like the stars in the night sky.

Of course, you can't see stars in the daytime. And many opportunities would never be noticed if things weren't black, if you weren't in a dark time of life.

So—do things look bleak? Is life dark? Hopeless? Then you're in luck. You're in the perfect position to spot the stars . . . new opportunities . . . fresh possibilities.

So get out the telescope and scan the skies. If you look for them, you'll find them. Ask for help, if you need it. Call someone who knows the territory, consult the manuals. Look, look, and keep looking. There's a star somewhere with your name on it.

FAITH IS ALWAYS STRONGER THAN FAILURE

Here's a powerful Power Thought. <u>Faith is always stronger than failure.</u> Faith is a way of life, failure is only a temporary condition.

The good news is that every successful person has known failure.

Henry Ford said, "Whew! I'm glad to have known failure. Now I can know success!"

If you have failed, admit it. Don't be ashamed of honest failure. The best way to handle the feeling of failure is with an honest but positive attitude. For it's impossible to fail without having been partially successful. You did succeed at overcoming the fear of getting started.

The world loves an honest person. If you have failed, be honest about it and admit it. Failure means that you're a human being. You made a mistake? We all make mistakes!

Good people will never give up on a courageous, honest person. They understand, they sympathize, they give you the strength and resources to start over. They never give up on you, unless you give up on yourself. Why should you give up on yourself? You've got too much going for yourself. Start believing in yourself again. That's the first thing you need to do. Choose faith, because faith generates hope, and hope always sees a star.

GET IN TOUCH WITH A CHILD TODAY

Where does God live? Where can you experience His spirit? Where can you and I find and feel and feed upon His Presence? Try connecting to someone who really radiates beauty. You will feel the reality of God when you choose to connect with one of His <u>special</u> persons, a little child. Have you ever prayed at the crib of an innocent, peaceful, slumbering baby?

Children are full of hope. You and I need to remain hopeful in a hurting world and the hope that is found in children is very good medicine.

So get in touch with a child. Go visit your grandchildren. Take time with your children today. Volunteer an hour or two a week in the preschool or children's department of your church. Forget that all-important appointment—reschedule it and call your teenager or naughty little son or daughter and enjoy them. Get into their world. That will give you the power surge to grab hold of life again.

Children have a wonderful way of always seeing the best in everything. You can learn so much from them. Adopt their worry-free attitude. Children are God's gift to us. When a new baby is born, anywhere in this world, it's God's way of saying that He hasn't given up hope for the human race. He still has high hopes for His human family!

Looking for Buried Treasure

There's no thrill like the thrill of making a great discovery. God hides the greatest treasures in the places we least expect.

It was only thirty years ago that the golden Buddha was discovered in the city of Bangkok, Thailand. For years, this huge, old concrete statue of Buddha sat in the middle of town. People put empty cans on it and used it to hold packages while they changed film in their cameras. Then one day while the statue was being moved, it cracked. Inside the concrete was the world's largest chunk of gold! That statue was eight feet high—solid gold.

A solid gold statue of Buddha! Centuries before, people afraid of being overrun by the enemy melted their gold pieces and created this statue, then covered it with cement, and floated it down the river. They were all killed, but the safely hidden gold statue remained a secret for centuries in the streets of Bangkok. Until one day, a priest asked if he could have it, and put it into his new, little temple.

As workmen started to raise it with a crane, the rope broke. It fell and a crack appeared on the chest. The next morning, with the rising sun, shafts of sunlight reflected off the gold hidden in the crack. The treasure was discovered. That statue was eight feet high—solid gold.

God conceals His treasures in our thoughts. Those positive thoughts are nuggets of gold. Don't be surprised if something breaks and you discover the hidden beauty in the broken place.

"ACT GLAD TO SEE ME"

I was signing books a couple of years ago. I looked up and there was a young girl who handed me her book to sign. She was maybe twenty years old. I was impressed with her, because I liked the button she was wearing. The button said, "Act Glad to See Me."

What would happen if we all acted glad to see each other? Think how you would feel if every person you met treated you like they were glad to see you.

Every person is a link. That link is important. I don't know if we'll ever know how important that link is. When you meet someone, remind yourself that they are here for a very special purpose, just like you are. Every person you meet has great possibilities.

Keep a positive attitude about every person you meet. He or she may be the one that will make all the difference in your life.

How large is your circle of friends? What kind of a friend are you?

"A true friend is someone who believes in you after
he has seen you at your worst."

Look for friends who believe in you. God says, "Act glad to see me," for God is that kind of a friend. He believes in you even at your worst times.

PUT YOUR HEART INTO IT

I don't gamble, but I love horses. And when I can, I like to watch the Kentucky Derby. I'll never forget a horse in the Derby called Sunday Silence.

Sunday Silence was an amazing animal. That horse should have been dead twice. As a colt, Sunday Silence got colic. If you know anything about horses, you know that a colt with colic rarely survives. Sunday Silence got colic as a colt and survived. But that was only the start.

He was put up at two separate auctions. Nobody wanted him. There wasn't a single bid made for that horse. Then he was almost killed when the driver of the trailer he was riding in had a heart attack and there was a terrible accident. Sunday Silence didn't even break a leg.

Finally, Charles Widdingham bought Sunday Silence, sight unseen, for $25,000. Charles Widdingham was seventy-six years old, the oldest trainer ever to bring a horse to the Kentucky Derby. The rider, Pat Valenzuela, had just been rehabilitated from drug abuse. Most people wouldn't have bet one dollar on this horse, his rider and his trainer.

But Charlie and Pat worked with this horse. They trained him. They worked with him. Why? Everyone thought they were crazy, wasting their time.

The day of the first race arrived. When the horses came out of the gate, there was Sunday Silence. He couldn't even run in a straight line. He was wobbling back and forth like he was confused. All of a sudden, it was if he realized, "I'm in a race! I want to win!" For Sunday Silence straightened up and took off like a shot. He won the race and he went on to win the Kentucky Derby.

201

Now horse trainers will tell you to look for the horses that have heart in them.

I believe in people who have heart in them, because I know it's just a matter of time. I see in them what can be, and what will be—they are a grand possibility!

BUILD A DREAM AND THE DREAM BUILDS YOU

Most people don't know this. It's true. Build a dream and the dream builds you.

Walt Disney had a dream to make feature-length animated motion pictures. In the 1930s this was unheard of. No one had ever done it before.

Walt went ahead and started making *Snow White and the Seven Dwarfs.* He spent millions of dollars building that dream. In the 1930s, millions of dollars was an incredible amount of money to spend on a movie. Before it was over, Disney spent more money on *Snow White and the Seven Dwarfs* than other studios had invested in *Gone With the Wind* and *The Wizard of Oz* combined.

Disney hired hundreds of artists—animators he called them. Good animators are rare; their work requires flawless artistry combined with vivid, creative imagination. By the time he was halfway through the project, the ranks of the Disney staff had increased to over a thousand.

Disney allowed nothing to stand in the way of his dream. He knew he was on to something. If a technique or camera didn't exist for what he wanted to do, the Disney people invented one.

Disney began work on *Snow White* in 1934. The film was released to critical acclaim four years later, in 1937. The rest, of course, is history.

If not for *Snow White*, there would be no *Pinocchio,* no *Peter Pan,* no *Bambi,* no *Beauty and the Beast.* There would be no Disneyland. All these dreams were built by the dream *Snow White and the Seven Dwarfs.* Disney invested every dime he had, and borrowed from every one he could borrow from until they said, "No more." He made the dream he called *Snow White* come true.

That was his dream. Look what it built for him when he built the dream.

What's your dream? Don't be afraid to start building it. Start right now. Do something to get your dream going today.

Put the cornerstone down. The sooner you do, the sooner it will build you.

I WOULD IF I HAD

Write down this statement right now.

I would_____, if I had _____.

The secret to this is not to write down: I could if I had. That's wishful thinking. Think "I Would"—that's one step away from positive action. "I would" is making a promise to succeed. Make a promise to yourself to make your dream come true.

I would if I had_____. WRITE IT DOWN.

I would buy a new house if I had a buyer for my old house.

I would expand my business if I had two more investors.

I would submit my design if I had more confidence in myself.

Now put it someplace where you will see it often. Take a look at it. Read it over and over to yourself. You're one step closer to success. You've written your dream down and identified your need. Now fill your own deepest need, your dream.

Look at your dream again. Is it true and honest? Is it what you really want? Is it clear and concise? What would you dream if you knew you would succeed? If you knew there was no way in the world you could fail, there was no obstacle you couldn't overcome, what would you dream?

Start dreaming this way. BIG! As big as you can.

The only difference between "great" people and "ordinary" people is the size of the dreams they've committed their lives to.

SAY "YES" TO YOUR DREAM

What one thing would you do if you knew you could not fail? Write it down in capital letters. Don't be afraid that what you write down will be silly. Humor relaxes you. When you're relaxed, you're free of the stress of being too serious. Now you can think creatively. Let your imagination run wild.

Take a look at what you've written down. Do you know what you've just created? Do you know what's staring you in the face right now?

Opportunity!—with a capital O. That's opportunity you're looking at. There's an open door right in front of you. Through that door is where your dream comes true. Through that door is success.

You can bet Walt Disney wrote down *Snow White and the Seven Dwarfs*. He saw that as clear as day. Then he said *YES!* to it. He gave it the green light. He said *YES!* to Disneyland, too, when no one else believed in him. By believing in himself, he gave himself the green light.

Now give yourself the green light. Look at your paper in front of you. Look at your dream. Now write one more word under it. Make the letters bold. Three little letters—one huge, positive response: Yes! Say "Yes" to the opportunity.

Say "Yes" to your dream!

OBSTACLES ARE
OPPORTUNITIES IN DISGUISE!

Look for the positive in every obstacle. There is good in everything. Focus on the positive. That's where the opportunity is. It's always in the positive.

Chuck Norris is a hero to many kids, including my grandchildren. He has fought with Bruce Lee and many of the world's top karate champions and come out on top. He has starred in many action films. Chuck recently shared with me the obstacles he has had to overcome in his life.

"Believe it or not, I was so shy in high school that I could never go up in front of the class and give a report. I took an F because I was scared. Today I'm a movie star.

"I tell people not to quit when they come up against an obstacle, because that obstacle could be the opportunity to make your dream come true. That one obstacle could be the one that makes it all happen for you, and you'll never know it until you overcome it.

"There are thousands of kids who are just like I used to be. They don't have the strength to believe in themselves. That's why so many kids get into trouble these days, because they don't have faith and strength. I like to tell them that there is hope out there. There is a way. It begins when you start to believe in yourself, then find somebody who'll give you the guidance.

"Have faith in God. You'll never achieve success in life without having faith in God.

"When you start to have this faith, positive things start to happen in your life."

WHEN THE GOING GETS TOUGH—LAUGH!

What do you do when you've painted yourself in a corner? Laugh! Laughter solves a lot of problems. Laughter reduces tension and helps you regain control. Most of the problems you encounter in life aren't that serious. Things are always much better than you think they are.

I have a friend who lost tens of millions of dollars in the recent recession. I ran into his wife recently. I said, "Jane, how are you doing?"

I expected to see her eyes fill up with tears. But, do you know what she did? She laughed.

"Things are tough! We're not sure if we're going to be able to keep our house. That's all we have left and we haven't made a mortgage payment on it in months."

She was grinning from ear to ear as if she was telling me she'd just won the lottery. I had to know what she was thinking. I had to know how she could be so happy when their life was in financial ruin.

"What is it? How do you do it, Jane? I mean, you look and sound like you're on top of the world!"

She laughed, "People think I'm crazy. They actually think I don't know what's going on. They've said, 'You don't get it, Jane!'

"But I do get it, Dr. Schuller! I truly believe we'll get back on our feet someday. In the meantime we have had to rely on God and on our Possibility Thinking faith—and it's been great! We've learned so much about ourselves and have gotten into Bible study. We never would have learned those great things about ourselves if we were still financially on top of the world.

"Well, I've got to go." She gave me a quick hug and a broad smile. "Bye-bye, Dr. Schuller!"

Laughter solves a lot of problems because it gives you a more positive outlook. Change your outlook and you will change your life.

"I WILL NOT QUIT"

When I was in my junior year of college I returned to my boyhood home for the summer break. I looked forward to seeing my mother and my father, and to being on the farm again.

I welcomed the fresh air and the simple pleasures of just being home and enjoying Mom's deep-dish apple pies.

That summer a tornado destroyed our farm. It was completely destroyed! Our house was ripped right off the foundation, swept up into the sky and smashed against the earth. The trees, roots and all, were pulled out of the ground. All the animals were killed. The crops were all gone. Twenty-six years of sweat and hard, steady work were wiped out in less than ten minutes. Ten minutes. It was a total loss.

To make matters worse, the mortgage was due. Now there was no way my father could pay it.

The neighbors, whose farms were also destroyed, quit and moved on but not my dad. He took the insurance check for three thousand dollars and marched down to the bank. I went with him. The banker was astounded when my father told him he was making a mortgage payment.

"But you need this money to buy new equipment and to rebuild," the banker said. "We'll manage," my dad said. "I'm making the mortgage payment." The banker so admired my father's faith that he rewrote the loan. He wanted to help.

We bought an old house, took it apart and rebuilt it on our farm. Within five years, my father had paid off the entire mortgage and was more prosperous than he had been his whole life. He made it because he held on.

I will never forget my father's holding-on power. "I

WILL NOT QUIT!" was his slogan day after day, month after month, year after year. Now each time a problem comes along, I remember how he held on and came out a winner!

When it looks like it's all over, hold on! Things are going to get better. They always do, if you'll just believe.

HAVE AN "I BELIEVE IT" BOX

I have an executive friend who keeps an "I Believe It" box on his desk. He swears by its effectiveness.

It's a cardboard box he found in the trash can one day. It's just a plain white cardboard box with a lid on it.

On the box he wrote the words *With God All Things Are Possible.*

"Whenever I get a project that just won't move forward," he told me, "or that I need a little extra help with, I put it in the box, close the lid and work on something else. I've put everything you can think of in there," he adds with confidence. "I've put in sales contracts that no one could fill, proposals that couldn't get funded, ideas that could never get off the ground. Once when I was having marital difficulties, I even put my marriage certificate in there. It always works.

"That 'I Believe It' box really works. Sometimes I don't take the item out for weeks at a time, other times I take it out the next day and I take a new look at it. Somehow, I see something I didn't see before. I think of a new way to attack the problem. I jot it down, and if it still doesn't move where I want it, back in the box it goes. It always works. I have never lost one sale, one project or proposal, and my marriage is stronger than ever."

Do you have an "I Believe It" box? Tape the message "With God All Things Are Possible" to the front of your in-basket, and watch what happens.

You'll be amazed at the results you get.

Always Look for the Positive

Train yourself to always look for the positive. Always look for the best in every person you meet, every negative thought you have, every obstacle you encounter. Once you find the positive, you will move forward, and you will move quickly.

Surround yourself with positive people. Positive people are successful, and when you surround yourself with positive people, you surround yourself with success.

What are the marks of positive people?

They are energetic. They look you in the eye when they talk to you. They are honestly enthusiastic and they are quick to compliment you. Positive people have a great faith in themselves and others. They are self-confident, self-assured.

Positive people are naturally cheerful and happy! It's fun to be with them. You feel better when you're with them. Positive people walk with their shoulders back and their heads held high, looking for new and exciting opportunities.

Positive people quickly volunteer their help, dedicating themselves to their church or their community.

Today, look for the positive in yourself, too. Dress a little sharper, walk with more purpose in your step. Hold your head up a little higher today. Those are all signs of a positive, moving-forward person. The world needs more positive people. The world needs more people like you.

213

PARALYZED BY FEAR? LET YOUR FAITH RELEASE YOU

Fear is the enemy of faith. Fear controls you, manipulates you, and fills you with self-doubt. These negative forces soon paralyze you and you find you can't function well at work, at home or in society.

Financial experts use the phrase "paralysis analysis." This is when you analyze something until it paralyzes you. You become so confused and scared after all your analysis that now you don't know what to do—paralysis analysis. That's real <u>fear</u>! Now try faith. Fear paralyzes you. Faith releases you.

Visualize your success. Focus on what you want to happen instead of being afraid of what might happen. Focus on positive things happening to you.

Close your eyes and take a deep breath. Take the deepest breath you can. Feel fresh, new life coming into your lungs. Now blow out all tension and exhale all fear. Visualize warm waves gently lapping on the shore. Feel the tranquillity of water flowing through lush gardens. Now be quiet for a long time. Arrange a quiet time each day. Things aren't going to get any worse during these moments. So enjoy this time alone. Your fears are fading fast.

Now, end your meditation with these words:

Heavenly Father, I don't know what is happening to me right now, but I know you have a plan for me—a plan for good and not for evil; a plan with a future and a hope. I believe in you, Lord.

I Believe—with God All Things Are Possible

Don't let your faith be shaken by life's difficult experience. When the obstacles you encounter are bigger and stronger than you've ever experienced, then you need an inrush of divine power. When you come up against a mountain too big for you, ask God for help. If God is for you, what could possibly be against you?

Here is a power thought to strengthen your faith for the tough times:

I believe with God all things are possible. (Matthew 19:26)

If you work out regularly (I run a few miles a day), and are pushing forward to some set goals, try this: Write down the words *I believe with God all things are possible* and tape them on your weight machine, inside your locker, or on the handlebars of your exercise bike. Write the words in big, bold letters and put them in a place where you will read the sentence regularly.

These words are some of the most powerful words in the Bible, a great source of faith and love. People read the Bible more than any other book and they live with the power of the great promises found there. *With God all things are possible.* This one, short sentence will put positive power into your faith.

God is real. He believes in you. If you want God to work in your life, you have to believe in Him. When you say, *I believe with God all things are possible*, you're exercising obstacle faith.

215

Do you have faith? Look beneath you. The chair hasn't fallen out from under you, has it? That's Faith.

Now tap into its power. You can be anything you believe you can be when you believe in a God who can make all things possible.

Believe and succeed.

BELIEVE IT—OR NOT!

I was on a radio talk show recently and somebody telephoned in and said:

"Dr. Schuller, I'm an atheist. I think you're wrong and as soon as you're dead you'll know it." He laughed and I heard myself say, "You know, if thirty seconds, or make it ten seconds, before I die, I got the message, irrefutable, totally convincing, 'Schuller, you got ten seconds to live and you're gone. You blew it. There is no God. There is no heaven. There is no hell. You made a big mistake!' I would say, 'Oh, am I ever glad I lived the way I did. If I had to do it all over again, I'd embrace the same faith. I'd preach the same sermons. I would trust the same God. I wouldn't change a thing, because it did so much good for my life. I was able to live with hope instead of despair, with faith instead of fear, and with optimism instead of pessimism. And that made me such a much nicer guy than if I had never believed. Oh, I wouldn't have changed a thing, and that's the honest-to-God truth.'"

It's a scientific rule that when something produces continual positive results, that something is real—whether you believe it or not!

DON'T MISS THE BEST THINGS IN LIFE

Are people ignoring you or no longer inviting you to be a friend? Take a long look at yourself in a magnifying mirror. New wrinkles on your face? Worry lines around your eyes? Signs of aging? Yes, but they also could be the result of warning signs of negative and complaining thoughts.

The humorous story is told about an Italian monk who went to the monastery at Montserrat in Spain. One of the requirements at Montserrat was perpetual silence. The monks were only allowed to speak after two years, and then they were permitted to say only two words. After two more years went by, they were allowed to say two more words, and so on. Two years, two words.

After the first two years had passed, the new monk was called before his superior to make his first two-word statement. The monk's first two words were "Bed hard."

Two more years passed. His next two words were "Food bad." Another two years passed and his words were, "I quit!" The superior looked at him and said, "Doesn't surprise me. All you've done since you've been here is complain, complain, complain."

Life is short. We miss the best things in life when we spend our time complaining. But watch out, for complaining quickly becomes a negative habit. Then we only hurt ourselves. Today focus on the positive, not the negative. Let's decide not to complain today, but rather let's compliment!

Don't miss the best things in life.

FACE YOUR FEARS AND FAITH WINS OUT!

When we moved to the home where we live now, we discovered that the people next door had three Doberman pinschers. The huge dogs welcomed us as soon as we moved in. Dobermans are marvelously beautiful creatures, but they are very ferocious. When I did my morning running, they would see me, and as soon as I ran past their fence, they would come racing after me, teeth bared, foaming at the mouth.

Later, I noticed how my little girl would walk over and play with the little neighbor girl. My little girl would play alongside of the Dobermans, but the dogs would never bother her. I kept saying, "Honey, you'd better watch out for those big dogs."

"Daddy," she answered, "those dogs are trained."

"I know they're trained," I would say, "but please be careful."

Then she told me the secret. "Daddy," she said, "you just don't understand. Those dogs are trained only to bite someone who is running away. That's why they never bother me. I never run away from them."

Oh.

Most, if not all, fears are the kind that we run away from. Fear is trained to strike at our hearts only when we run away from it. Face fear, and you'll find that you're not really afraid after all. You're just standing in the shadows as I was with the Dobermans. Face what you fear most and it will fade away.

FILL A VITAL NEED

Find a need and fill it. What are the vital needs of the people where you live? What product or service can you provide that would fill that need? What can you do that no one else is doing?

I categorize the basic needs of people as follows:

1. Food, clothing and shelter
2. Security
3. Family and friends
4. To understand and be appreciated
5. To help others
6. To find God

Every person has these basic needs. Companies and businesses have similar needs. Providing a service or product that fills a need starts you on the road to success. Look around you. There are always countless unfilled needs in every community.

Think positively and identify a specific need that is unfilled. Match this to your own unfilled needs. Chances are, the unfilled need in your community matches up with a need in yourself. Find this need and fill it, and you will be a success!

PLAN FOR SUCCESS

This may sound pretty basic, but the fact is most of us don't take the time to plan for success. Most of us plan for failure, because if you fail to plan, you plan to fail. Today, take time out to plan for success.

If you expect good things to happen, they will. If you plan for success, you'll get it. Fix firmly in your mind the thought of achieving your goal. See yourself winning the award, reporting a profitable business year, getting letters from satisfied customers, expanding to a new location, taking that well-deserved vacation.

Sit down and write out a plan. Make it as detailed as possible. Make the plan neat and easy to review. A good plan for success is priceless. You can't spend enough positive time making a plan for success.

After you have finished your Plan for Success, sign it. Write a sentence or two promising that you will make this plan happen. You will dedicate yourself and your resources to the endeavor. Then sign it, make a copy and put it somewhere you will see it often.

I have known many people who have made great plans, but they were not successful because they would not personally commit to making the plan happen. Don't make this mistake. Dedicate yourself by signing your own name to the plan with words of commitment.

Remember: Plan your work—now!—Work your plan.

Play the
"Wouldn't it be wonderful if . . . " Game

When you get an idea that immediately says, "Wouldn't that be wonderful if that were possible?," write it down. You may be on the edge of a great opportunity.

Developers use this method of discovery all the time. Wouldn't it be wonderful if people could do most of their shopping in one place instead of driving all over town? That's how the mall concept was born.

Wouldn't it be wonderful if people could pay less and get more? That's how membership warehouse clubs became so successful.

Play the "Wouldn't it be wonderful if . . . " game for fifteen or twenty minutes. See what you come up with. Take a drive around your town and look around. What do you see that you can do that would be wonderful if it could be done? You'll find something wonderful that you can do.

My mother made the best deep-dish apple pies. When a neighbor or someone else in town needed help, my mother would quickly put on her old, faded apron, pare the apples and roll out the pie dough.

An hour later, the aroma of cinnamon and baking apples filled the house. Then she would quickly take off her flour-dusted apron and what a sparkle she had in her eyes as she would walk out the door with her wonderful apple pie.

She knew she had done something wonderful!

TURN YOUR OBSTACLES INTO OPPORTUNITIES

Today remind yourself to expect setbacks. There will be obstacles in your way. There will be problems you have to solve. Expect them.

Plan to stall. That's a sign of good management and wise leadership. No one goes from Point A to Point B without adjusting their course a little bit. Always know that you can solve any problem, you can overcome any obstacle, because you know that anything is possible!

You've got a dream, you've found a need to fill, and you're moving forward. You know there are going to be times when you have to take a step back, and that's okay. You expected this.

Today is the day to turn all your obstacles into opportunities. Look for the positive in your obstacles. There is good in everything. Solving problems motivates and strengthens your belief in yourself.

Look for blessings disguised as problems and you'll move forward.

TALENT IS SPELLED W - O - R - K

Is it good news or bad news that talent is spelled W-O-R-K? The bad news is that we wish talent could just be handed out without any effort on our part, and that success is something that just falls into our laps.

Say the word "work," and people quickly lose interest in their dreams.

The good news is that when we change our attitude about work, we begin to enjoy it.

Question: When is work "fun" and "fun" work? What's the difference between "fun" and "work"? Everything anyone does for "fun" someone else will do for "work."

I find it fun to spend a day fishing, but the fisherman who earns his living that way day after day quickly finds that the sport of fishing becomes very hard work.

Recognize that Talent is spelled W-O-R-K.

Work isn't drudgery to the Positive Thinker.

Work is an opportunity to contribute something positive to the world.

When you do your work cheerfully, you are well on your way to success.

"I BELIEVE! I BELIEVE! I BELIEVE!"

When I'm called as a pastor to people in times of great tragedy and trouble, I share these miracle-working words with them:

"I believe! I believe! I believe!"

I first learned this exercise from Dr. Daniel Poling, the prominent clergyman from Marble Collegiate Church on Fifth Avenue in New York City. Dr. Poling was Norman Vincent Peale's predecessor.

During World War II, Dr. Poling's son died at sea when he went down with his ship. He was one of the chaplains who gave up his life jacket to a crew member.

In his grief, Dr. Poling found the courage and renewed faith to continue his work through this exercise: He repeated aloud again and again these miracle-working affirmations:

"I BELIEVE! I BELIEVE! I BELIEVE!"

Even if the words don't come naturally, force yourself to repeat them morning, noon and night. Force them into your subconscious. These words will give you the power to face life again. I guarantee it!

ITEMIZE YOUR ASSETS

Today make a list of all your assets. In a business this is a quantification of your cash reserves, machinery and equipment, investments and employees. Don't forget about your people. People are the top and bottom line of every business.

At home, make a list of all the good things you have. Such as:

1. I have shelter. (I didn't have to sleep under a bridge last night.)
2. I have food to eat. (I do not have to raid the garbage dumps or beg for food today.)
3. I have loved ones who care for me. I am not abandoned or forgotten.
4. I have the freedom to dream, to set goals and attempt to do something wonderful with the life I have.
5. I have the faith to face all my tomorrows.
6. I have work to do. I have the mental and physical ability to work.

Things always look better when we remind ourselves of the good things we already have.

Now list your liabilities. If your liabilities are more than your assets, you are near bankruptcy and you need a big inrush of positive faith. Focus on all of your positive assets, and give all of your liabilities to God. He is always able to balance the bottom line!

BE A WINDOW AND A MIRROR TODAY!

One of the greatest honors I ever had was when Mother Teresa asked me for a copy of the Crystal Cathedral prayer in my handwriting: *Lord, let my life be a window for Your light to shine through, and a mirror to reflect Your love to every person I meet.* After I wrote it out for her, she tucked it in her tunic, close to her heart.

The Crystal Cathedral windows (all 10,760) are made of a glass which allows the congregation seated within to see the sky, the birds, the clouds, the trees. Those outside the cathedral see only 10,760 mirrors reflecting the same clouds and trees . . . and they see themselves.

When the Cathedral was dedicated, I wrote these words and they became not only my prayer but a prayer of dedication that people everywhere around the globe are living out—in India, with Mother Teresa; in Southern California, with my baseball-playing grandson; with Sweet Alice in Los Angeles or John Croyle in his homes for troubled children.

Repeat the prayer: *"Lord, let my life be a window for Your light to shine through, and a mirror to reflect Your love to every person I meet,"* and watch the power flow from your life.

THINK! THINK! THINK! THINK! THINK!

I stopped to see a dear friend on a recent trip through Chicago. I owe him so much not only for all of his wise advice through the years, but also his trust in me when I was too young to prove I would accomplish any lasting ministry.

His slogans and sentences really pushed me forward. His name: W. Clement Stone. His motivating spirit continues to influence my thinking and my work even today. Often I hear him say with the voice of a commanding General, so strong, so certain of this classical truth:

"What the mind can believe you can achieve!"

He believed and expanded this power thought!

I listened to many of his platform speeches and each time his closing persuasive advice to the thousands of young people was dramatically carried out as he walked from the podium, off the stage, disappearing, his voice still ringing out bold and strong:

THINK! THINK! THINK! THINK! THINK!

What power is released in our lives when we take the time to think!

TEAM UP FOR SUCCESS

The greatest successes are seldom accomplished by one individual. The bigger the dream, the bigger the team needed to make it come true. Never underestimate the importance of teamwork.

Freedom to plan, freedom to dream, freedom to imagine—these are all the necessary requirements for teamwork. Freedom generates maximum energy and extracts unbelievable dedication.

Nothing stifles creative thinking quicker than the subconscious anxiety of having your creative ideas rejected by your spouses, your boss, your coworkers, your staff or yourself.

My wife and I are a great team. We share our dreams, our projects and our work. As the Bible says in Ecclesiastes 4:9, "Two are better than one."

Team up with some of the finest brains, some of the most talented people in our country today. These people probably work right beside you or live in the same house you do. Develop a working climate of great trust and liberty.

Facing a difficult task today? Team up with someone who has the ability to help you.

Team up for success!

FIX THE PROBLEM, NOT THE BLAME

We all make mistakes. However, one of the biggest mistakes you can make is to fix the blame and not the problem. John Wooden, the famous coach of the UCLA basketball team, once said, "No one is defeated until he starts blaming someone else."

Each of us has the power to make any problem we have better or worse. Choose a positive attitude toward fixing the problem and you will avoid falling into the trap of fixing the blame.

Many people become threatened when they are blamed for problems. Whether the problem is their fault or not, when you continue to blame people, you are only fixing the blame, not the problem.

When you fix the blame, you are actually making the problem worse. Threatened people become angry people. Angry people will not help solve the problem. Only positive, calm people can help solve the problem.

Go through the whole day today without fixing the blame. Approach every problem from overhead with a positive outlook. Look for the real cause of the problem and focus yourself on coming up with a positive, long-lasting solution.

SHARE THE CREDIT

God can do great things through the person who doesn't care who gets the credit.

You will be more productive if you learn to share the credit. People who willingly invite others to get involved in their project are always more successful.

Sharing the credit comes under the principle of positive giving. Whatever you give away will always come back to you. When you share the credit, great things happen. A cure for disease, a breakthrough in the development of a new product, a new scientific discovery are all made possible when you share the credit.

Be a team builder, not an empire founder. Empires crumble; teams go on to win championships. The challenges facing us as we approach the twenty-first century are demanding great teams that are willing to share the credit. These are the teams that will be able to solve the problems of tomorrow.

NEVER MAKE AN IRREVERSIBLE
DECISION IN A DOWN TIME

That's a mouthful, isn't it? Memorize this: *I will never make an irreversible decision in a down time.*

Don't let your emotions make your decisions. Don't let your temper rule your life. Tough times pass. Tough people survive.

Every company, every person, every family, every job has its down times. Recognize when you are in a down time. Are you ill? Are you filled with grief? Have you just had a terrible argument with your spouse? Someone insulted you? Frustration, depression and anger usually are prevalent in a down time.

Be careful. Don't make any major moves. This is the time to be careful. Rest. Wait. Now is not the time to make an irreversible decision.

Be patient. Never make an important decision when you are in a bad mood. Cool off. Your feelings will change, I promise you, and they will be more positive than the ones influencing you in a down time.

Negative motions result in bad decisions during down times. Reserve your judgment until the sun is shining. Never make an irreversible decision in a down time.

TREASURE TIME LIKE GOLD

We all tend to waste what we value too lightly. Every successful person knows the truth in the words "Time is money." Think of the time you have each day as a bar of gold.

You can invest this bar of gold wisely or squander it wastefully. Properly invested, your time can be used to generate new ideas, organize plans, invent new products, study problems, acquire knowledge or gain new experience. These activities all lead to higher levels of achievement.

Have you ever noticed people who seemed to lack energy, while others tend to move fast and seem to abound in energy? Work each day as if it were your last. This will rapidly increase your tempo of achievement. It will also increase your energy supply.

Treasure time. Most successful people I know are the ones who waste no time getting started on a project or even a new career. Adopt the Do-It-Now Principle. Why not? Successful people do it. Do the same and you will be more successful than you ever thought you could be.

Get started—today!

God's Love Blooms When We Love Each Other

What a beautiful day it is today, all over the world. You know, no matter where you live, no matter what your condition is, it's a beautiful day because you are alive and you can experience a beautiful mix of moods coming into your consciousness.

Your personality is undergoing a process constantly. And it's affected by the thoughts that you allow to have dominance in your mind. Your personality is constantly reflecting happiness, joy and positive moods, or discouragement, depression and down moods. It's up to you to make the choice. Today, I invite you to make a decision to be enthusiastic, upbeat, positive and happy.

Do you want to feel the love of God today? Do you want to experience the reality of the love of the eternal God Who created the world with its trees and birds and flowers and people? Do you want to really experience the reality of a relationship with God?

Then, here's how to experience God. Find someone, touch them. Pick up a telephone, talk to somebody. Reach out and touch someone. Be concerned, care, encourage, affirm. Tell somebody how wonderful they really are. They need that encouragement. And God's love will bloom inside of you as you reach out and encourage someone else.

Yes it's really true, God's love blooms when we love each other.

8

Power Quotes
for
Power Thinkers

Here are the <u>Power Quotes</u> from my pen and person. These one-line messages are part of a collection from forty-three years of ministry.

At the end of a news conference recently, a news reporter shot this question to me: "How do you want to be remembered? What do you want on your tombstone?" My immediate reply was "I want it to be remembered that I was an encourager!"

May these Power Quotes encourage and empower you for LIFE. Come alive and really live!

• Great things happen when God and you confront a mountain!

• For every mountain there is a miracle.

• Never judge reality by your limited experiences.

• It takes but one positive thought when given a chance to survive and thrive to overpower an entire army of negative thoughts.

• A possibility thinker never votes "no" to an idea that holds some possibility for good.

• Let your imagination release your imprisoned possibilities.

• Let the "gonna's" get you going!

• You will never win if you never begin.

• The most tragic waste is the waste of a good idea.

• Success without conflict is unrealistic.

• Your greatest asset is YOU!

• Possibilitizing is overcoming while you're undergoing.

• If you don't have dreams beyond your grasp, you've already begun to die.

• Let your dreams, not your regrets, take command of your life.

• You can often measure a person by the size of his dream.

• Faith is spelled R-I-S-K!

• God matches the dreams to the dreamers.

• Make sure your dreams are big enough for God to fit in.

• God's dreams are always so large that they require His help to make them come true.

• The only place where your dream becomes impossible is in your own thinking.

• Courage is spelled I-N-T-E-G-R-I-T-Y.

• Nothing great ever happens on the O.K. level.

• Never let a problem become an excuse.

• There's no hopeless situation until you become a hopeless person.

• If there exists no possibility of failure, then victory is meaningless.

• God + me = A majority

• If you listen to your fears, you will die never knowing what a great person you might have been.

• Storms always lose to the sun. The sunrise always overtakes the night . . . and winter always turns into spring.

• Impossible situations can become possible miracles.

• Abandon the "if only's" and substitute "however" or "at least" or "next time."

• May you WANT as long as you live!

• Capitalize on your crisis!

• When it looks like you've exhausted all possibilities, remember this: You haven't!

• Always look at what you have left. Never look at what you have lost.

• When you feel you're at your lowest, remember this: "There is nowhere to go but UP!"

• Never allow a fractured experience to shape your future.

• Add up your joys and never count your sorrows.

• If you're creative enough to imagine a problem, you're clever enough to discover a solution.

• Don't trust the clouds . . . trust the sunshine!

• Selfishness turns life into burdens. <u>Selflessness</u> turns burdens into life.

• Press on. Obstacles are seldom the same size tomorrow as they are today.

• Turn your hurt into your halo.

• Today's accomplishments were yesterday's impossibilities.

• God believes in you and He can't be wrong!

• The opposite of Pride is not humility—the opposite of Pride is shame.

• The "I Am" will always determine the "I can."

• Yesterday's responsibilities are tomorrow's possibilities.

• Let your hopes, not your hurts, shape your future.

• The Peak to Peek Principle: Climb the mountain and catch the new vision.

• The "I've Got It" must never catch up with the "I Want It."